Casebook on School Reform

Casebook on School Reform

Edited by
Barbara Miller and Ilene Kantrov

HEINEMANN

Portsmouth, NH

Heinemann
A division of Reed Elsevier Inc.
361 Hanover St.
Portsmouth, NH 03801-3912
Offices and agents throughout the world

© 1998 Education Development Center, Inc.
All rights reserved. No part of this book may be reproduced in any form or by electronic or mechanical means, including information storage and retrieval systems, without permission in writing from the publisher, except by a reviewer, who may quote brief passages in a review.

Library of Congress Cataloging-in-Publication Data
Casebook on school reform / Barbara Miller and Ilene Kantrov, eds.
    p. cm.
  Includes bibliographical references
  ISBN 0-435-07246-3
  1. School improvement programs—United States—Case studies.
2. Teacher participation in administration—United States—Case studies. 3. Educational change—United States—Case studies.
4. Case method. I. Miller, Barbara II. Kantrov, Ilene.
LB2822.82.C374   1997
371.2'00973—dc21   97–23939
                                                                                             CIP

Editors: Leigh Peake, Scott Mahler
Cover Design: Darci Mehall
Manufacturing: Louise Richardson

Printed in the United States of America on acid-free paper
01 00 99 98 97 DA 1 2 3 4 5 6 7 8 9

CONTENTS

ACKNOWLEDGMENTS *vii*

1 **INTRODUCTION** *1*
   Why Use the Case Method? *1*
   Why a Focus on School Reform? *2*
   Where Did These Cases Come From? *4*
   How Are the Case Materials Structured? *4*
   How Might the Cases Be Used? *5*
   Conclusion *9*

2 **OLIVER'S EXPERIMENT** *11*
   The Case *12*
       Nancy Cali, Barbara Miller, Ilene Kantrov, and Cynthia Lang
   Facilitator's Guide *17*
       Nancy Cali, Barbara Miller, Ilene Kantrov, and Cynthia Lang

3 **ALL ABOARD?** *23*
   The Case *24*
       Nancy Cali, Barbara Miller, Ilene Kantrov, and Cynthia Lang
   Facilitator's Guide *29*
       Nancy Cali, Barbara Miller, Ilene Kantrov, and Cynthia Lang

4 **WHERE DO WE GO FROM HERE?** *35*
   The Case *36*
       Jessica Richter and Cynthia Lang
   Facilitator's Guide *45*
       Deborah Bryant, Jessica Richter, and Cynthia Lang

5 ALMOST THERE—OR ARE WE? *51*
   The Case—Part I *52*
      Jennifer Nichols, Ilene Kantrov, Jan Ellis, and Cynthia Lang

   THE CASE—PART II *63*
      Jennifer Nichols, Ilene Kantrov, Jan Ellis, and Cynthia Lang
   Facilitator's Guide *67*
      Jennifer Nichols, Barbara Miller, and Ilene Kantrov

6 DROPPING A STONE IN THE WATER *75*
   The Case *76*
      Deborah Bryant and Barbara Miller
   Facilitator's Guide *80*
      Deborah Bryant and Barbara Miller

7 WHAT DO WE MEAN BY "SCALING UP"? *89*
   The Case *90*
      Melinda Fine, Barbara Miller, and Ilene Kantrov
   Facilitator's Guide *101*
      Deborah Bryant and Barbara Miller

   BIBLIOGRAPHY *111*

ACKNOWLEDGMENTS

Many people have contributed to the development of the cases in this book through their interest, enthusiasm, and advocacy of cases as an important professional development tool. For their support, we want to acknowledge Charles Thompson, Linda Alford, Joan Hunault, Toby Bornstein, Peggy Funkhouser, Lavaun Dennett, Carolee Matsumoto, Thom Clark, Jackie Mitchell, Judy Kemp, and Mark Driscoll. The case authors (Nancy Cali, Cynthia Lang, Jessica Richter, Jennifer Nichols, Jan Ellis, Deborah Bryant, and Melinda Fine) brought their thoughtfulness and creativity to the task of constructing compelling case narratives.

A number of people helped us to create a book out of the individual cases. We want to thank Myles Gordon and Cynthia Lang for their encouragement in compiling this book. Deborah Bryant was a careful and critical reader of all the cases and offered suggestions that strengthened each one. Lisa Christie was persistent and creative in securing permission to use the cases in this book. Cynthia Grzelcyk provided invaluable administrative support throughout this project. Leigh Peake, as acquisitions editor at Heinemann, never wavered in her conviction that this would be an important and useful book. Her interest and support over the long course of this book's development were very helpful to us.

1

INTRODUCTION

Cases are becoming an increasingly popular format within the field of education for structuring conversations around challenging issues. This casebook represents another contribution to that field. The most powerful cases are more than narratives of events; they are cases "of something" (L. Shulman 1992, 17). They represent some larger set of ideas and therefore are worthy of reflection and deliberation. We believe that a well-crafted case "of something" is like an evocative photograph that captures a subject, invites multiple interpretations, and is rich enough to sustain repeated encounters. Good cases have that same kind of complexity, drawing the participant into the topic and evoking comparisons to other experiences. Much of the current case literature in education provides snapshots of complex and contextualized classroom interactions, focusing on the effectiveness of different curriculum materials, assessment strategies, or teaching techniques. There is also, though, a need for rich cases that address the challenges of school reform. The cases in this book focus on the issues that arise when teachers, administrators, and the larger community engage in efforts to reform their schools and districts.

WHY USE THE CASE METHOD?

The case method is a useful approach to bring out, explore, and change beliefs as well as to expand knowledge. Having said that, it's important to note that there is no "industry standard" by which the case method is described or evaluated. While most educators writing about the case method trace its origins to the use of cases in law, business, and medicine (Kleinfeld 1992; Merseth 1992; Sykes and Bird 1992; Doyle 1990), there is no consensus within the education field about what constitutes *the* case method (L. Shulman 1992) or *the* context for case use (Kagan 1993). Most agree that the development, use, and facilitation of cases open opportunities to analyze and reflect on difficult issues as they emerge in a particular setting and to apply the resulting insights to one's own situation (J. Shulman 1992; Barnett and Sather 1992; L. Shulman 1986; Sykes and Bird 1992; Wassermann 1993). Further, most concur that the power of cases is magnified when they are used by a group, as a catalyst for discussion (Barnett, Goldenstein, and Jackson 1994; Shulman and Mesa-Bains 1993; Kleinfeld and Yerian 1995; Silverman, Welty, and Lyon 1992). Participants can, in the company of others, analyze the various problems embedded in a case, work to generate and evaluate alternative solutions, and discuss and reflect upon the underlying issues.

Use of cases in this fashion resembles the kind of good teaching advocated by most current school reform efforts. The call is for teaching that encourages multiple perspectives on a given issue, emphasizes critical thinking, and explores various answers and approaches. When cases are used most productively, they support this kind of teaching and learning. Teachers who participate in case discussions, whether in preservice or inservice settings, experience for themselves the kind of teaching and learning dynamics that they wish for their own classrooms.

Moreover, we believe that the case method makes a considerable contribution to the creation of a community of learners among education professionals. Cases such as those in this book are typically used with groups of educators. Because of their complexity and open-ended nature, they invite different perspectives and provide an opportunity for educators to articulate and consider various viewpoints. With a focus on the analysis of problems and reflection on issues, educators have the chance both to reflect on their own experiences and to hear one another's ideas. Whether fictional or drawn from life, cases such as those in this book offer a realistic but less personal and therefore less threatening vantage point on difficult issues. Using cases in the company of colleagues, educators can begin to imagine and work together toward new kinds of actions, different interactions, and changed expectations.

WHY A FOCUS ON SCHOOL REFORM?

In this book, we offer cases of school reform, more specifically, cases that investigate different aspects of school reform: What is the nature of collegiality that supports reform? How is consensus for reform built across the school and larger community? What are the ramifications across a district when schools engage in reform? These cases, we believe, offer important windows into the challenges of school reform by focusing attention on different aspects of the process of change.

The language of school reform is part of the vernacular in education today. In many schools and districts it has become a catch-all phrase that encompasses the majority of new initiatives, from school management councils to curriculum standards and frameworks. Yet many of these reform efforts do not live up to their initial promise. Designed to implement sweeping changes, many efforts are short-lived and local.

Part of the explanation for this limited impact lies, many claim, in the underlying assumptions about the process of change. Michael Fullan has written about the chronic tendency among those engaged in reform to underestimate the magnitude of the effort required to reform schools and to overlook the inherent conservatism built into educational systems (Fullan 1993; Fullan and Miles 1992; Fullan and Steigelbauer 1991). As a result, many change efforts suffer from an inadequate understanding of the problems at hand as well as from a reliance on superficial solutions. Another aspect of the limited impact of school reform efforts can be linked to a prevailing focus on structural changes, such as increasing the length of a class period or instituting site-based management (Elmore 1995; Elmore 1996; Cohen 1995; Tyack and Tobin 1994). The implicit assumption is that reform of school structures will result in changes in teaching and learning, and therefore lead to improved student performance. Many reformers have looked to specific structural changes as *the* innovation that will start the chain reaction of school reform. However, such approaches rarely address the mediating factors that link school structure and the core of educational practice.

Taking such critiques of reform efforts to heart, we have through the case format focused on the multiple perspectives and interacting factors that characterize change within schools. We see the process as inherently complex, involving many different facets, so we provide in these cases as much of that larger context as we can. These are not Aesop's fables, in which the moral of the story is laid out, to be emulated in real life in real schools. Instead, these cases are narratives of what happens as teachers, administrators, students, parents, and others attempt to change some fundamental aspects of practice. While believing that the core of educational practice, the kind of teaching and learning that is at the heart of effective schools, should be connected to structural features, we don't aim a spotlight on the new policies and their attendant structural changes as though they were the stars of the show. Rather, we also illuminate the more mundane and ultimately more important attitudes, expectations, and mindsets of those who work day to day in schools and districts, so that those who are using these cases can reflect on the nature of school reform in its complexity.

WHERE DID THESE CASES COME FROM?

The cases in this book were written for different funders, to meet different needs, and to be used by various audiences. The cases are all fictionalized accounts of events. They were developed through a process of data collection, including interviews with individuals who have encountered similar school reform challenges, but the characters and story lines are composites. As indicated in the introduction that precedes each case narrative, the organization that commissioned the case had a hand in framing the case and also offered feedback during the case's development and initial use, which helped to ensure that the case accurately reflected the essence of the circumstances from which it was drawn and did not unfairly portray any real people or situations. However, these cases are not documentary accounts of individuals or events within a particular organization or project.

Staff from Education Development Center (EDC), Inc. worked with each organization to develop the case and facilitator's guide. EDC is an international nonprofit organization dedicated to promoting human development through education. Founded in 1958, EDC now maintains more than two hundred projects in the United States and throughout the world. The scope of the organization's work reaches from math and science curricula to school health, from environmental education to systemic school reform. EDC specializes in designing and implementing training programs for a wide range of workers and professionals, but particularly for teachers and school administrators.

HOW ARE THE CASE MATERIALS STRUCTURED?

This book contains six sets of case materials. Each set includes a brief introduction, describing the genesis of the case and its original purpose. The cast of characters is presented, along with any terms that may be unfamiliar to the reader. The case narrative follows. Each set of case materials concludes with a detailed facilitator's guide, offering background information on the case and its major issues, and a sequence of activities for guiding the case discussion.

Some of the cases have study questions at the end of the case narrative. These questions may be used for individual reflection prior to discussion, and most of them are present in the activities outlined in the facilitator's guide. Exhibits that accompany some of the cases offer different kinds of information about the case issues.

Each of the facilitator's guides utilizes a similar structure. Background information, including a synopsis of the case and a list of its major school reform issues, is offered to orient the facilitator to the case. Following this is a section titled Guiding the Discussion, which contains a variety of discussion questions and activities. The case facilitator is encouraged to use judgment in structuring the case experience for participants. Facilitators may use the discussion questions and activities in the order presented in the guide, they may choose to reorganize the activities, or they may substitute activities from other facilitator's guides. Across the six facilitator's guides a range of activities is described, and a character analysis activity from one guide may be exactly what a facilitator is looking for in discussing another case. Each facilitator's guide has some common discussion questions, including defining the central problem in the case and considering next steps. However, each case also offers distinctive sets of questions to guide exploration of a particular school reform issue.

Each facilitator's guide offers some tips for facilitating a productive case discussion. Some guides are more directive than others; some offer more details in structuring groups or orchestrating discussion. The assumption is that the discussion of these cases is a group activity, so some kind of public recording of the conversation, through use of overhead transparencies, flip chart paper, or black or whiteboard, is important. Case facilitation offers exciting opportunities for skill development and learning on the part of the facilitator. We encourage you to read *A Guide to Facilitating Cases in Education* (Heinemann, 1998) by Barbara Miller and Ilene Kantrov, for an extended discussion of the strategies, skills, and decisions that go into effective case facilitation.

HOW MIGHT THE CASES BE USED?

Each of these six cases is set in a different location with a distinct cast of characters and offers a particular vantage point on issues of school reform:

"Oliver's Experiment." Oliver, a classroom teacher, changes his assessment strategies, with ramifications for parents and his department.

"All Aboard?" Three teachers develop effective strategies for working with Limited English Proficiency students and face the challenge of engaging their principal and colleagues in their school.

"Where Do We Go from Here?" A principal and her faculty work to make and sustain substantial changes in their school's structure and mission.

"Almost There—Or Are We?" A group of teachers, administrators, and parents face the complexity of creating school-based curriculum change.

"Dropping a Stone in the Water." Teaching colleagues from across a district encounter the systemwide ripples that emanate from their actions to change their instructional practices.

"What Do We Mean By 'Scaling Up'?" Teachers, principals, community members, and state personnel experience the challenges of sustaining innovation and extending work to new sites.

While you may choose to use only one of the cases, we encourage you to consider how the six cases could be used in an extended inservice or preservice curriculum. Taken as a set, these cases can be used in a variety of ways.

Characters

You may choose to focus on school reform issues through the eyes of a particular character, such as a teacher or principal. Figure 1.1 indexes the cases in terms of their active characters. For example, all six cases feature teachers, and the cases might be used in sequence to reflect specifically on the role and concerns of teachers in school reform efforts. Or you might focus on the principal, and therefore choose the four cases that feature a principal. Working with a group on these four cases, particularly with some of the discussion questions about principal leadership from the facilitator's guide to "Where Do We Go from Here?" is one option. By choosing to focus on a particular character, you can use these cases to direct participants' attention to the roles and responsibilities of a teacher, principal, or other key player in school reform.

Settings

You may want to order these cases by setting, focusing on the different venues in which school reform issues are played out: classroom, school, district, and state; Figure 1.2 shows how these six cases cover the range of settings. You might begin with "Oliver's Experiment," the case most closely identified with school reform issues at the classroom

CHARACTER	CASE					
	Oliver's Experiment	All Aboard?	Where Do We Go from Here?	Almost There— Or Are We?	Dropping a Stone in the Water	What Do We Mean by 'Scaling Up'?
Teacher	X	X	X	X	X	X
Department chair	X			X		
Principal		X	X	X		X
District staff				X		
Parent	X			X		X
Community Member				X		X
University/ state/ project staff					X	X

FIGURE 1.1 *Characters*

level, and then use the other five cases, ending with "What Do We Mean by 'Scaling Up'?" which frames school reform issues as part of a state initiative. Or you could choose cases that you and the group see as featuring the most challenging settings for school reform issues. For example, a group working on the districtwide implications of school reform would find that "Dropping a Stone in the Water" and "Almost There—Or Are We?" offer good opportunities to reflect on and discuss issues they face in their own sites.

Issues

You may organize these cases by a logical development of ideas about achieving school reform, as illustrated in Figure 1.3. Here the cases are organized so as to move from one set of ideas to another, taking the opportunity to focus on a particular school reform issue with each case. Beginning with analysis and inquiry into the nature, pace, and scope of change with "Oliver's Experiment," this organization of the six cases builds a common understanding of related ideas about school reform, culminating in consideration of large-scale reform efforts as presented in "What Do We Mean by 'Scaling Up'?" Or, if you and the group have a shared base of experience and knowledge about the nature of change and the importance of collegiality, you might choose to begin with cases

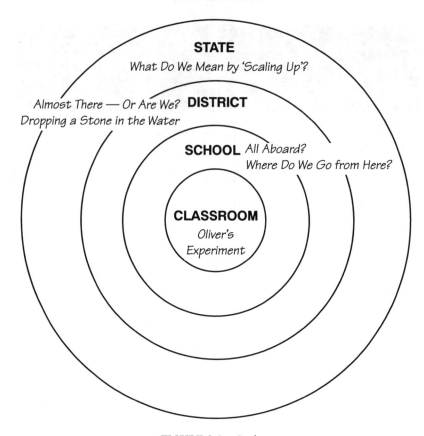

FIGURE 1.2 *Settings*

CASE	SCHOOL REFORM ISSUES
Oliver's Experiment	Nature, pace, and scope of change for an individual teacher
All Aboard?	Collegiality and dissemination of good practice
Where Do We Go from Here?	Leadership and collaboration to change school structures
Almost There—Or Are We?	Community consensus building around curricular goals
Dropping a Stone in the Water	Systemwide implications of instructional changes
What Do We Mean by 'Scaling Up'?	Building greater buy-in and reaching greater numbers as scale-up options

FIGURE 1.3 *Issues*

that highlight collaboration and consensus building on a larger, more complex scale, such as "Where Do We Go from Here?" and "Almost There—Or Are We?"

CONCLUSION

We offer these suggestions for ways of using the cases to stimulate your thinking, not to offer a prescribed agenda. As we have noted, there is no consensus about how best to use cases in education. In fact, some of the excitement of cases is in how varied and rich different discussions of even the same case can be. We find that each group that uses a case generates new insights and looks at the information in the case from different perspectives, so that even the authors of a case may be surprised at what others find in it.

A metaphor we have used elsewhere (EDC/EES 1995; Miller, Kantrov, and Hunault 1996; see also Style 1988) helps to identify the source of this variety and to capture an essential value of cases. Cases can serve as both a *window* into the experiences and ideas of the educators portrayed as they grapple with key issues of school reform and as a *mirror* of the beliefs and attitudes of those who read and discuss the case. Participants in a case discussion reflect on and discuss what they see through the window of the case—the actions, issues, and characters that they find engaging. Participants also consider and talk about what they find reflected in the mirror of the case—their own reactions to what they see and what those reactions tell them about themselves and their own circumstances. Working in a group setting, people learn how what appears through the window of the case is reflected differently in others' mirrors. Case discussion therefore tends to highlight the variety of ways in which different people see, experience, and interpret the world.

We hope that the richness and diversity of perspectives stimulated by discussing these cases can deepen understanding of the issues they address and spark creative efforts that take into account the complexities of the reform process.

2

OLIVER'S EXPERIMENT

In 1993 the Los Angeles Educational Partnership (LAEP), a public education fund, commissioned Education Development Center to develop two cases for its School-Wide Change Project within Los Angeles area schools. This initiative consisted of seminars and on-site assistance for teams of teachers, administrators, and parents committed to creating curriculum-based changes in their schools. The cases reflect the complexity and challenge of classroom change efforts, particularly the schoolwide implications of those changes. The cases were intended to offer users opportunities to reflect upon, discuss, and resolve critical reform issues.

"Oliver's Experiment" is about change from the perspective of an individual high school teacher as he works to bring his mathematics curriculum, instruction, and assessment in line with the National Council of Teachers of Mathematics' *Curriculum and Evaluation Standards* and other reform guidelines. The case also considers the teacher's relationships and communication with other individuals (a parent, a fellow teacher, and a department head) and looks at how their different perspectives, interests, and concerns can affect a teacher's attempt to change.

The characters and events described in "Oliver's Experiment" are fictional, although the case does represent real issues and challenges encountered by teachers in Los Angeles and elsewhere involved in schoolwide change efforts. The development of this case was funded by LAEP.

Characters

Oliver Wright, mathematics teacher at Grove High
Leti Ramirez, student in Oliver's geometry class
Jovita Ramirez, mother of Leti
Bill Chamberlain, mathematics department head at Grove High
Lucy Dobbs, mathematics teacher at Grove High

Glossary

California Mathematics Framework. Curriculum framework in mathematics for the state of California, describing what students should know and be able to do at various grade levels

CLAS tests. California Learning Assessment System, open-ended problems and enhanced multiple-choice test items linked to the *California Mathematics Framework*

NCTM *Standards.* Standards in mathematics for curriculum, instruction, and assessment developed by the National Council of Teachers of Mathematics

Off-track. Time when various groups of teachers (and students) are on vacation at year-round schools

THE CASE

Nancy Cali, Barbara Miller, Ilene Kantrov, and Cynthia Lang

Oliver Wright held the classroom door for Jovita Ramirez, wondering what had moved her to come in for a personal conference. Parent involvement at Grove High School was still highly unusual, even though faculty members had recently intensified their efforts to increase it. He offered her a chair and sat across the table from her. Mrs. Ramirez cleared her throat, but then said nothing. Oliver tried to help her get started. "So, Mrs. Ramirez, you said over the phone you'd like to talk with me about Leti's math work?"

Mrs. Ramirez looked pained, but determined. "Yes, Mr. Wright, I did. I know it's only early November, and maybe Leti still has to get used to you, but I'm very worried. Leti was bringing home A and B tests last year. She liked math and was good at it. Last Friday, she brought home a test with a C on it." Mrs. Ramirez laid the test on the table between them. "Leti never gets C's in math."

Oliver smiled inwardly, Is this all? The Lake Wobegon effect strikes again—all parents want their kids to be above average. "I understand your concern, Mrs. Ramirez. But let me say that a C is not really a bad grade. In my class, a C means that a student can demonstrate her understanding of basic mathematical concepts and can use those concepts and her thinking skills to solve simple problems."

"But Leti says she *doesn't* understand. She doesn't know what you want from her. I don't really, either," Mrs. Ramirez continued, tapping her finger on the test. "They have to work with each other on one of these problems? Leti said she had to spend ten minutes just explaining this problem to the other students in her group. And you ask her here to *write* about how she solved the problem. And here, in question five, you tell her to solve the problem in *two different ways*? What is all of this for? Math wasn't like this when I went to school. Why can't you give her normal tests like the ones she had last year? She understood how to study for those. She did well on them."

As Oliver listened to Mrs. Ramirez's descriptions of the test, he realized how foreign it must look to the average person. He had to admit that it looked pretty different to him, too. Aloud, he explained to Mrs. Ramirez that he was trying to respond to research that had shown that "normal" multiple-choice tests didn't assess many of the important skills that students needed to learn and didn't allow them to use the range of skills that they brought to their understanding of mathematics. He told her about the NCTM *Standards*, California's CLAS tests, and the school's decision to examine its assessment practices.

Mrs. Ramirez didn't seem reassured. "If you don't give her regular tests, she won't pass the tests for college. She might not get a scholarship. She wants to go to college. *We* want her to go to college. She *has* to do well on those tests. And I'm afraid that you're not preparing her for them."

"I hope that that's not true, Mrs. Ramirez. I think that as Leti gets better at complex thinking skills and at communicating her thinking to others, she'll also improve her ability to do well on standardized tests." Oliver realized that he sounded as if he were trying to convince *himself*.

"I don't know. . . . Are all the tests going to be like this? Are these scores going to count towards Leti's grade?"

Oliver felt a momentary surge of panic. He didn't really *know* whether he was going to count this test's scores in figuring the students' grades. It was all so new to him. "Well, that's a good question. Sometimes, we assess students to find out how we're doing, so we can teach them better. I'm trying something new, and I hope I'm learning from it as much as the students are. As long as this new assessment is in its experimental stage, I'll certainly keep that in mind when grading the students."

"Well, Mr. Wright, I don't think you should be experimenting on my daughter. What if your experiments don't work? What if Leti doesn't get into college because she gets bad grades and low test scores because of your experiments?"

Oliver did his best to reassure Mrs. Ramirez that he wouldn't allow Leti to fall behind or get lost in math. They ended the meeting with an agreement that they would talk again after Leti's next test.

"I always said I wanted more parent participation," Oliver thought ruefully after Mrs. Ramirez left. "And now that I've got it I don't like it!" He felt depressed and troubled. He was perplexed by his reaction—he'd had a few really antagonistic meetings with parents, and they hadn't bothered him nearly as much as this one. Gradually, he realized that Mrs. Ramirez's visit had uncovered a lot of his own discomfort and uncertainty about what he was doing. He knew that getting feedback from others was important, but it was hard to hear his own doubts voiced by Mrs. Ramirez.

It was time to ask himself some important questions that he had avoided until now: What do I really believe? Are the changes I'm trying to make really worth all this trouble? What is it that I really want to accomplish, anyway?

Background

Bill Chamberlain, the mathematics department head, was one of the people who had influenced Oliver to try some changes in his assessment practices. In the abstract, Bill believed in the reforms advocated by NCTM and the *California Mathematics Framework*. They made sense to him, and it was clear that they were being widely accepted as the new direction for school mathematics. His own classroom practice, however, continued to be traditional more often than not.

Bill and the other department heads at Grove High School, after many discussions among themselves and with school administrators, had concluded last year that it was time to look at testing and assessment practices in the school in light of the state's CLAS tests and the current reform movements. As a result, Bill had sent a brief memo to Oliver and the other mathematics teachers in June, asking them to "think about the new ideas in assessment put forth in the *Standards* and the *California Framework*" and to "examine how they were assessing their students."

Oliver had taught mathematics for seventeen years and thought he was pretty good. He'd developed entertaining demonstrations of some mathematical concepts and theorems, and had an easygoing lecture style that created a comfortable atmosphere in the classroom. Students knew he was always available after school for them. Over the past few years, though, he'd noticed that more students seemed to be trying hard but were really struggling, or were tuning out. Their fundamental understanding of mathematics seemed weaker every year. He wanted to do more for them, if he could. So when Oliver saw Bill's memo, he took it seriously. He spent some of his off-track time in July and August reading about alternative assessment and its impact on curriculum and instruction.

It was really because of his conversations with Lucy Dobbs, though, that he had launched his experiment in curriculum and assessment this September. Oliver smiled as he remembered his conversations with her. Thinking about Lucy always made him smile.

From the first day she joined the faculty of Grove High School a year earlier, Oliver had been impressed by Lucy's enthusiasm and energy, her creativity, and her knowledge of cutting-edge mathematics and education research. She quickly acquired a reputation among students as a great teacher. She and Oliver struck up a friendship. Often they ate lunch together, talking about mathematics, about their work, and about the particular joys and frustrations of teaching.

One day in September, Oliver and Lucy started talking about Bill's memo and Oliver's readings about alternative assessment. "I know that it's important to assess our kids differently," Oliver said, "and it's all tied up with teaching them differently, but I'm not sure I'm up to it. The logistics of giving them open-ended problems, having them work together, making them write about their thinking—that's all pretty new to me. I used to stand at the board and demonstrate a proof, and I'd look out and see maybe five confused faces. Now, I seem to see *twenty-five* confused faces. I want to reach those kids, but I don't really know if I can change the way I teach after all this time. Old dogs, you know. . . . "

Lucy laughed and said she thought he probably had a few tricks left in him. She also sympathized with him, remembering her own beginning attempts to craft mathematics lessons built on the students' own experiences and prior knowledge. "It wasn't a picnic! Half the time I felt completely lost, and I couldn't see or plan beyond how I was going to get through the day. But I started noticing that kids were getting drawn into the math in a way they hadn't been before. I realized how valuable their own ideas—even their mistakes—were in learning mathematics well, and how much more interested they seemed to be in working at it."

Lucy described one unit on geometry and architecture that had really excited the students. It had taught them a lot not only about geometry and architecture but also about how to ask their own questions and create multiple solutions to problems.

Oliver asked whether he might try it with his students.

"Of course you can!" Lucy found her lesson plans and gave them to him. "If you can't read my chicken scratches, or you just want to talk over some ideas, you know I'd love to help."

In early October, Oliver started the unit with his geometry students. He soon realized that active investigation, working and talking with classmates, writing, and thinking creatively about mathematics were as new and uncomfortable for them as they were for him. Still, he saw new glimmers of excitement and engagement in the students. The assessment that he conducted at the end of the month—the one on which Leti had gotten a C—showed that both he and the students had a good deal to learn about this new way of doing mathematics. While Oliver found it even more challenging than he had expected, he was encouraged by signs that he was reaching more of his students. They seemed more animated in class, and they were talking to one another more about mathematics and less about dates and video games. He had been pleasantly surprised several times by students' unexpected and insightful questions or unconventional solutions to problems. They were showing more interest and persistence, and more imagination in their work.

What Next?

Oliver's feelings of encouragement had now evaporated in the face of Mrs. Ramirez's questions and his own. He thought it would be really helpful to talk with Lucy, but she had recently gone off-track and was out of town. Oliver then decided to talk with Bill and get his perspective and guidance on what the math teachers should be doing to "think about the new ideas in assessment" and to "examine how they were assessing their students," as Bill had suggested in his memo. The day after Mrs. Ramirez's visit, he dropped by Bill's classroom.

"I didn't realize how many issues would start coming up when I tried to change something," he explained to Bill. "I thought I was just trying to get the kids more actively involved in the math, but now I'm worried about how to grade them, how to make cooperative groups really work, whether I even know how to teach them to communicate mathematically and think creatively, whether I'm doing them a disservice by not testing them in the usual way. I haven't felt this unsure since I was a first-year teacher."

Bill shook his head. "This is something you're going to have to figure out for yourself, Oliver. I can't tell you what to do. If you believe in the *Standards* and in alternative assessment, then you're going to have to make the changes. It's not a bad idea, with the CLAS tests coming. But you're going to have to figure out the way that's best for you. Personally, I think going slowly is the key—doing one thing at a time. That way you can be really sure of what you're doing."

Oliver walked out of Bill's office lost in thought and torn between two desires. He wanted to back off, and he wanted to forge ahead. He wanted to act with Bill's conservatism and caution, but would changing his practice "one thing at a time" make enough of a difference for his students? He wanted to have Lucy's boldness, but was it right to try something he wasn't sure about or comfortable with? He hadn't forgotten why he had tried something different in the first place: He wanted to help *all* his students understand and appreciate mathematics. But he just didn't know anymore what to do next.

Study Questions

1. What is this a case of?
2. What should Oliver do next? Why?
3. What support does Oliver have in his attempt to change his practice? What additional support, if any, does he need?

FACILITATOR'S GUIDE

Nancy Cali, Barbara Miller, Ilene Kantrov, and Cynthia Lang

Synopsis of Case

Oliver Wright, a mathematics teacher at Grove High School in Los Angeles, feels he isn't reaching many of his students and turns to an innovative colleague, Lucy Dobbs, for help. Oliver eventually decides to try teaching one of Lucy's units on geometry and architecture.

After assessing his students using a test that, like the unit itself, requires them to work together, find multiple solutions to problems, and communicate mathematically, Oliver is confronted by a concerned parent who fears that her child's tests will adversely affect her child's grades, ability to do well on standardized tests, and ability to get into college.

Oliver, disturbed by his meeting with the parent, realizes that he feels many uncertainties himself about the changes in curriculum and assessment that he has attempted. After talking with his department head, he isn't sure whether to revert to his usual teaching practice or to continue trying new things.

Major Issues

The purpose of this case is to promote discussion about issues that arise when an individual teacher decides to make significant changes in teaching practice. The case is designed to engage participants in thinking about various dimensions of change, including

- Reasons for attempting change, both personal incentives and external motivations
- Supports for and barriers to change
- Pace and scope of change
- Images of successful change

Guiding the Discussion

Discussion of this case and of the issues it raises can proceed in different ways, depending on the needs and experiences of the discussion participants. The five sets of questions offered here provide several ways to structure a conversation around issues of educational change. The questions are not meant to be a script for the facilitator and are certainly not exhaustive; they are intended only to suggest *some* of the questions and issues that might be fruitfully pursued.

1. Describing the Situation helps participants to articulate their perceptions of the problem described in the case and to uncover differences and similarities in their perspectives.
2. Exploring Contributing Factors asks participants to consider the many factors, internal and external to the main characters, that shape this particular case.
3. Articulating Possible Next Steps gives participants the opportunity to generate and analyze possible actions that the central characters could take.
4. Replaying the Case invites participants to think creatively about the case and to suggest different actions the characters could have taken that might have caused the case to evolve differently (and for the better).
5. Looking at the Bigger Picture helps participants consider the broad issues of change involved, using the case as a springboard for discussion.

Several different discussions can be structured with these sets of questions. A few possibilities:

- A discussion that moves from consideration of the specific details of Oliver's situation to consideration of broader and more general issues of individual change would use questions from all five sections.
- A discussion that concentrates mostly on the larger issues of change would use the case as a springboard, moving quickly through sections 1 and 2 and spending most of the time on section 5.

- A discussion that focuses on Oliver as a "test case" would move quickly through sections 1 and 2, spend more time on section 5, and then return to sections 3 and 4 to apply the ideas discussed.
- A discussion that considers the case's major themes throughout would raise questions from section 5 as participants move through sections 1, 2, 3, and 4.

The study questions at the end of the case appear again in the following sections and can be used as a focus for individual reflection in preparation for the discussion.

1. Describing the Situation

What is the problem in this case? Whose problem is it?

How would each of the characters in this case describe the problem? How is it similar and different for each of them?

What feelings do you think the problem has raised for each of the characters?

2. Exploring Contributing Factors. What do you see as the factors influencing Oliver and his actions in this case? Factors might include

- The students' needs
- Oliver's growing awareness of the limits of his teaching approach
- Goals of the mathematics reform movement, as expressed in the NCTM *Standards*, the *California Mathematics Framework*, and so on.
- Oliver's relationship with Lucy and knowledge of her teaching practices
- Bill's memo regarding assessment strategies
- Oliver's knowledge of the eventual implementation of CLAS tests

What are some factors influencing the other participants' behavior and attitudes in this situation? Factors might include

- Parents' awareness and understanding of mathematics reform
- Students' and parents' expectations about grades and assessment
- Bill's meetings with other department heads about assessment
- Lucy's own experience with classroom change

What are other factors, not discussed in this case, that may have influenced the situation and Oliver's experiment? Some possible factors:

- Professional development opportunities (or the lack thereof) for Oliver and his colleagues
- Students' understanding (or lack thereof) of what Oliver was trying to do

  Encouragement (or lack thereof) from administrators for teachers' experimentation with new teaching methods and content
- Assessment practices beyond the school (e.g., college entrance exams)
- Mandates from the school district or the state concerning curriculum, instruction, scope and sequence, and so on

3. Articulating Possible Next Steps. What could Oliver do next? Some possible next steps:

- Oliver could back off completely and return to his former methods of teaching and assessment, which are more comfortable and predictable for him.
- Oliver could talk to Lucy, explain his situation and feelings, and ask her for advice.
- Oliver could ask for Mrs. Ramirez's help in forging a partnership with parents to explore and implement changes in mathematics curriculum and instruction.

What implications might each possible next step have for Oliver and his students? How might it improve or worsen the situation?

4. Replaying the Case. What might Oliver have done differently at any point in the story? How might it have changed the evolution or outcome of the case? Some possible ideas:

- Oliver might have gone to Bill before actually initiating the changes to ask for suggestions and help in how to proceed; Bill might have been more supportive later.
- Oliver might have focused in the geometry and architecture unit on only one new aspect, for instance, students' problem-solving skills, and emphasized these skills on the test; the assessment might have produced better results.
- Oliver might have arranged for Lucy or another colleague to observe his classes and give him feedback along the way, before the assessment; he might have anticipated problems and adjusted his teaching accordingly.

What supports or impediments might Oliver have encountered in each different scenario? What might other characters have done differently that would have changed the outcome of Oliver's experiment?

5. Looking at the Bigger Picture

Reasons for change. Oliver was motivated to try something new because of his own perceptions of his students' needs, Lucy's innovative teaching practices, and Bill's memo asking him to think about new ideas in assessment.

Was each of these influences beneficial to Oliver? harmful? neutral?
How does it matter if the impetus to change is internal? external? Does the impetus for change affect a teacher's perspective on change in general?
What, if any, factors are necessary to promote change by an individual teacher?

Support for and barriers to change. Oliver looked to both Lucy and Bill for support in changing his practice, with different results.

What was the nature of the support for Oliver's changing his teaching? Was it sufficient? What were the barriers that Oliver faced? Were they prohibitive?
What kinds of support are needed for educators to change their practice? Are there any conditions or supports that are *usually* necessary for change to be successful? How can they ensure that the needed supports are there?
What are the typical barriers to change that educators face? Are there any barriers that *usually* doom change attempts? How can those who attempt change circumvent or overcome barriers to change?
To what extent is an individual's past experience with change a support or a barrier to current efforts to effect change?
Is it possible for an individual to change successfully without others also changing? Does an individual have to enlist the support or understanding of others (colleagues, administrators, parents, students) in order to make change successful?

Pace and scope of change. By trying one of Lucy's innovative units, Oliver tried to teach and assess mathematics in ways that were new for him and for his students.

Would Oliver have felt differently about his efforts if he had altered the scope or pace of his changes?

Which changes are best done slowly? quickly? On what does the answer depend?

When is it best to attempt comprehensive changes? smaller or partial changes?

Images of successful change. While he was encouraged by what he was seeing among his students, Oliver's conversation with Mrs. Ramirez caused him to doubt his efforts.

How do you think Oliver would assess his efforts at change so far? How would you assess them?

In what ways are mistakes, false starts, or failures a part of change? How many setbacks are acceptable?

What are short-term markers of success that individuals need to identify when attempting change? How can teachers and others gauge the overall or long-term success of a change effort, in the midst of problems or uncertainties? Should they rely only on their own judgment?

In what ways are successful changes finished products? In what ways are they ongoing processes?

3

ALL ABOARD?

In 1993 the Los Angeles Educational Partnership (LAEP), a public education fund, commissioned Education Development Center to develop two cases for its School-Wide Change Project within Los Angeles area schools. This initiative consisted of seminars and on-site assistance for teams of teachers, administrators, and parents committed to creating curriculum-based changes in their schools. The cases reflect the complexity and challenge of classroom change efforts, particularly the schoolwide implications of those changes. The cases were intended to offer users opportunities to reflect upon, discuss, and resolve critical reform issues.

"All Aboard?" focuses on the dynamics of a small group of colleagues working together to develop more effective instructional strategies for the Limited English Proficiency (LEP) students in their third-grade classrooms. The case considers the issues that arise when small-scale changes are extended to a larger context, such as an entire school. In this way, the case provides a window onto the development of collegial relationships across a larger group or among an entire school faculty, and can be used to examine the benefits and difficulties of fostering schoolwide commitment to significant educational change.

The characters and events described in "All Aboard" are fictional, but the case does represent real challenges faced by Los Angeles teachers. Funding for the development of this case was provided by LAEP.

Characters

Anita Pascarello, third-grade teacher at Walker Avenue Elementary
Bibi Guzman, third-grade teacher at Walker Avenue Elementary

Helen Jordan, third-grade teacher at Walker Avenue Elementary
Kaye Vernon, principal at Walker Avenue Elementary

Glossary

LEP. Limited English Proficiency, a term used to describe students who receive school support services because English is not their first language

THE CASE

Nancy Cali, Barbara Miller, Ilene Kantrov, and Cynthia Lang

Anita Pascarello dashed into the teachers' lounge to grab her mail and a cup of coffee before school started. She was looking forward to her meeting with Bibi and Helen after school today. Their bilingual project, which had been underway for seven months now, was the most interesting team effort she had been part of in a long time, although lately they'd had very little time to talk about it. Anita had been completely absorbed in the last few weeks working with her parent volunteer and helping her students improve the peer tutoring they had begun in the fall. She was beginning to feel that she really was teaching differently, and better, and she was excited about being able to share some of the things that had happened in her class with her third-grade teaching colleagues. Unfortunately, they had all been so busy that they hadn't met for three weeks now.

Anita was surprised to find in her mailbox a memo written by Bibi to Kaye Vernon, their principal. Scrawled across the top was a handwritten note from Bibi: "Anita—Sorry I couldn't get this draft to you any earlier. I want Kaye to see this ASAP so we can get on the agenda for the April faculty meeting next week. What do you think? Bibi."

The Memo

To: Kaye Vernon
From: Bibi Guzman
Re: LEP Strategies Project

As you know, Anita, Helen, and I have been involved since October in trying out strategies that can help us work more effectively with our Limited English Proficiency students. We're really excited about the work we've done, and we feel that we've made important changes that are very positive for our students. We also think that we've developed a really powerful and effective way of working together.

We'd like to share our experiences with our colleagues at next week's faculty meeting. We would need about twenty minutes on the agenda. During that time we would talk about the following:

- How we got to this point, from Anita's initial question, Am I doing a good job with my LEP students? to our current question, How can other teachers here at Walker be doing a better job with LEP students?
- The strategies we're using that we think are really powerful: (1) recruiting parent volunteers to come into the classroom as language resources for LEP students, and (2) using peer tutors, where English-speaking students and LEP students work together one-on-one and in cooperative groups.
- The ways that Anita, Helen, and I have been working together on this project. It's the most supportive and positive collegial relationship I've had in a long time.
- The support you've given us, in encouraging us to try new things and to address the problem of working more effectively with LEP students.

We think that other teachers here at Walker have been struggling with some of the questions that we have faced—and solved! We want to share our strategies for LEP students and our method of working together as a model that our colleagues can adopt.

Please let us know as soon as possible about next week's agenda. We will begin planning our presentation while we wait to hear from you.

Anita laughed to herself and shook her head. Isn't that just like Bibi? To read this memo, you'd almost think that what we're doing is a piece of cake. She makes it sound as if we have all the answers, that working together is smooth sailing, *and* that we always know what our next steps should be.

Background

Walker Avenue Elementary School is a K–6 school in a working- and middle-class area of Los Angeles, serving more than 900 students. In the past, the school had a good reputation in its community and beyond. In recent years, however, some parents have started to complain that Walker "isn't what it used to be." Test scores are down, budget cuts have hurt staffing and the physical plant, and parent involvement is declining. The composition of the student population is changing faster than the school's ability to establish formal bilingual programs. Currently, many classrooms have LEP students with various levels of English fluency.

Kaye Vernon, the principal, came to Walker three years ago from an inner-city school and had a reputation for supporting teachers and promoting schoolwide changes. Kaye saw change taking place at Walker, but it often felt agonizingly slow and inconsistent. Each year, several individual teachers had started strongly, trying things like interdisciplinary units or hands-on mathematics lessons, but by December or January they had mostly reverted to their traditional curriculum and instruction. She knew that they often felt overwhelmed by the pressing day-to-day challenges of the classroom.

Anita was one of those teachers who was trying to bring about change in the classroom. This year, during the first few weeks of school, Anita had found herself worrying more and more about her LEP students. In her two years of teaching, she had become increasingly frustrated. She was certain that the LEP students weren't learning enough in *any* language, and she felt inadequate in her efforts to help them. She knew that this was not an issue only for her. To some degree, each of the thirty teachers at Walker was struggling with the needs of LEP students.

By mid-October, Anita's frustration had peaked. She concluded that she simply didn't know enough to reach her LEP students effectively. Overcoming her usual reticence, she resolved to ask Bibi for some help.

Bibi Guzman was one of the few classroom teachers at Walker who spoke Spanish, which she often used working with her Spanish-speaking students (although she, like Anita, also had LEP students who spoke other languages). Bibi used a rich, multicultural curriculum that she had designed herself. She was an energetic, passionate teacher who enjoyed talking and working with colleagues. Anita thought Bibi could be a good resource for a relatively new teacher like herself and hoped that Bibi wouldn't mind spending a little time talking to her.

Bibi was delighted to be asked, and suggested that they could pool their efforts to help the LEP students in *both* of their classes. "Let's get Helen and Evelyn in on this and make it a gradewide project. They're full of good ideas, too."

Evelyn Rogers, a popular veteran teacher, wished them well but declined to join them. "We all have our own ways of teaching. I like the way I teach, and I think I'm very successful at it. So do the parents. I don't feel the need to change what I'm doing. I'm happy to share what works well in my classroom, but I really don't have time to work with you on a long-term project."

Helen Jordan thought it would be pleasant to work with other teachers—something she had rarely done—so she agreed to join Anita and Bibi. She had developed a wide repertoire of teaching strategies over her twenty-six years of teaching and had been focusing in the last few years on teaching to different learning styles. Anita knew she would learn a lot from both Bibi and Helen.

Different Perspectives

As soon as the three teachers sat down for their after-school meeting that April afternoon, Bibi started talking enthusiastically about their presentation. "Just think of the other teachers that we can recruit! And once we have the parent volunteers and the peer tutoring rolling along, we can come up with even more ways for teaching our LEP students. I'll bet we can even get Evelyn involved."

"I think the other teachers would agree that we all have a lot to learn from one another," Helen responded mildly.

Anita's eyes drifted over Bibi's memo. "I don't know, Bibi, this makes me uncomfortable. Some of the most powerful things that happened for me over the past year aren't really reflected here." Anita paused. "I wonder if this is the way to go."

Bibi was mystified. "But why, Anita? We've been doing great things this year!"

Anita responded slowly, "I agree that we've done some great things this year, and it's not that I don't want to share our work with other teachers, Bibi. I do. But I don't know *what* we should share with others—or why."

"*This* is what we want to share," Bibi replied, pointing to the memo. "We should talk about the things we've accomplished and the impact they've had on our students. I know other teachers will want to hear about that."

"But it's not just *what* we've accomplished with our kids, it's *how* we went about our work that helped us to be as successful as we were," said Anita. "I remember one of our first conversations together, when we were in Helen's room and I was trying to put into words my concerns about the LEP students in my class. I wanted them to become proficient in English as fast as possible and still use and value their native languages, but I really felt lost as to how to do it, or why that was really important to me. After we had talked for almost two hours, I was astounded at how much I had figured out, with your help, and how important it had been to talk things through with the two of you."

"I remember that meeting, Anita," Helen commented. "You looked as if you had run a marathon by the time you were through! You really stuck with your questions, and I could see they were important. It made me realize that much of what I do with LEP students is kind of implicit."

Anita turned eagerly towards Helen. "Yes, exactly! And once we all started to talk through what kinds of curriculum and instruction would support LEP students, then I understood why you suggested peer tutoring."

Bibi laughed. "Well, you know that I think it's important to talk about things with each other. It's usually hard to get me to stop talking."

"But I think that it's more than just the ways we talk together," Anita replied. "I also think that we're really there for one another. In your memo, Bibi, you wrote that 'it's the most supportive and positive relationship I've had in a long time.' I think we have a very positive relationship, but it hasn't always been easy. For example, when we were talking about parent volunteers, it took some time and some compromising to come up with a game plan that worked for us all."

"And I remember," Bibi said, "telling you over and over, 'Don't worry Anita, all the details will work themselves out.' And they did! I knew you would do a great job, and you have."

"I appreciate your pushing me to 'jump right in,'" Anita said. "I don't know if I would have had the courage to try some of the things I've done this year if you two hadn't been there to encourage me to take some risks."

Helen commented, "I think that we've been able to help each other through the hard parts. I've found it really valuable to be able to try out ideas with the two of you and to get feedback."

Bibi frowned slightly. "So if we all think that we've done some important work together this year, what's the problem?"

Anita responded, "I guess I'm not sure what we'd be asking of the faculty in this presentation. It's true that some of the things we've changed in our classrooms this year have really helped our students. Are we asking that everyone do all the same things we did? We *have* worked out a productive and satisfying way of working together. Do we want everyone else to work in just the same way? I'm not sure we have this perfect method that everyone else can just '*adopt.*'"

Bibi smiled. "Of course people who collaborate are going to find their own wrinkles that need to be ironed out; that's to be expected. But if we've changed our practice by working together in ways that really help our students, don't you think we have an obligation to spread the word? Why should every teacher have to reinvent the wheel?"

Anita sighed. "I'm not saying we should keep it a secret. Maybe I'm just wondering whether people will appreciate our presenting our work as a model for them to follow. You know, we still haven't been able to get Evelyn to work with us."

Bibi answered, "Well, maybe not Evelyn—yet—but we certainly have Kaye on our side. She told me that she was thrilled to see that we really kept our momentum through the year. You know how many times she's said that working with LEP students is the biggest challenge we have here at Walker. And our working together is something that she's really supported. So, I still think the presentation at the faculty meeting is a good idea."

Anita looked across the table. "What do *you* think, Helen?"

"Well, I'm really not sure," replied Helen. "Isn't there something we can do that will satisfy all of us?"

Good old Helen, Anita thought to herself with a touch of exasperation, always looking for the middle ground. She looked from Helen to Bibi and asked, "So, what do we do next?"

Study Questions

1. What is the problem in this case?
2. What should Anita (and Bibi and Helen) do next? Why?
3. What do you see as the characteristics of working collegially to make change?
4. Are these characteristics the same when working with a large group or school faculty as when working with a group of three?

FACILITATOR'S GUIDE

Nancy Cali, Barbara Miller, Ilene Kantrov, and Cynthia Lang

Synopsis of Case

Anita Pascarello, a teacher at Walker Avenue Elementary School in Los Angeles, is frustrated by her attempts to help her Limited English Proficiency students and turns to her grade-level colleagues for help. For the rest of the year Anita, Bibi, and Helen work together on two different strategies—parent volunteers and peer tutoring—that can better serve the needs of their LEP students.

Bibi's draft memo to the principal, requesting that the three teachers make a presentation to the faculty about their work, causes Anita to realize that she and Bibi have different perspectives on what they have done together. The three teachers meet to discuss the proposed presentation and, in the course of the conversation, reveal different ideas about what is important in their collaboration and what it means to share their work with colleagues. Anita, Bibi, and Helen are left with questions about how they can be part of a schoolwide change effort.

Major Issues

The purpose of this case is to promote discussion about issues that arise when a teacher works collaboratively with others to make changes in classroom practice. Its premise is that substantive and long-term change is rooted in teachers' working collegially. Discussion of the case offers the potential for focusing on the nature of the collegial relationships among a small group of teachers and the changes they attempt together. In addition, it can raise questions about the process of fostering change among a larger group or across a school, and the role of collegiality in such an effort. The case is designed, therefore, to engage participants in thinking about various dimensions of collegiality and change, including

- Motivations and expectations for working collegially
- Nature of working collegially, in terms of creating professional relationships and negotiating conflict among colleagues
- Scope and pace of changes that are collegially driven
- Role of collegiality in supporting and sustaining change, especially schoolwide change

Guiding the Discussion

Discussion of this case and of the issues it raises can proceed in different ways, depending on the needs and experiences of the participants. The four sets of questions offered here provide several ways to structure a conversation around the issues of collegiality and educational change. The questions are not meant to be a script for the facilitator and are certainly not exhaustive; they are intended only to suggest *some* of the questions and issues that might be fruitfully pursued.

1. Describing the Situation helps participants to articulate their perceptions of the problem described in the case and to uncover differences and similarities in their perspectives.
2. Exploring Contributing Factors asks participants to consider the many factors, internal and external to the main characters, that shape this particular case.
3. Articulating Possible Next Steps gives participants the opportunity to generate and analyze possible actions that the central characters could take.
4. Looking at the Bigger Picture helps participants consider the broad issues of collegiality and change, using the case as a springboard for discussion.

Several different discussions can be structured with these sets of questions. A few possibilities:

- A discussion that moves from consideration of the specific details of Anita's situation to consideration of broader and more general issues of collegiality and change among small and large groups would use questions from all four sections.
- A discussion that concentrates primarily on the broader issues of collegiality and change would use the case as a springboard, moving quickly through sections 1 and 2, and spending most of the time on section 4.
- A discussion that focuses on Anita, Bibi, and Helen as a "test case" would move quickly through sections 1 and 2, spend more time on section 4, and then return to section 3 to apply the ideas discussed.
- A discussion that considers the case's major themes throughout the conversation would raise questions from section 4 as participants move through sections 1, 2, and 3.

The study questions at the end of the case appear again in the following sections and can be used as a focus for individual reflection in preparation for the discussion.

1. Describing the Situation

What is the problem in this case? Whose problem is it?

What would each of the characters in this case say the problem is? How is it similar and different for each of them?

What feelings do you think the problem has raised for each of the characters?

2. Exploring Contributing Factors.
What do you see as the factors influencing Anita and her actions in this case? Factors might include

- Growing needs of LEP students in the school
- Anita's desire to teach LEP students more effectively
- Dynamics of the working relationship among Anita, Bibi, and Helen
- Principal's support of teachers trying to change their classroom practice
- Community concerns about the school

What are some factors influencing the other participants' behavior and attitudes in this situation? Factors might include

- Bibi's eagerness to work with other teachers
- Helen's desire to try something new
- Kaye's experience in an inner-city school
- Evelyn's satisfaction with her teaching practices

What are other factors, not discussed in this case, that may have influenced the situation and the teachers' collaboration? Factors might include

- Professional development opportunities (or the lack thereof) for Anita and her colleagues
- District or public pressures to institute programs for LEP students

3. Articulating Possible Next Steps. What could Anita (and Bibi and Helen) do next? Some possible next steps:

- Anita could propose a presentation focusing on how the three teachers have worked together to make change.
- Anita, Bibi, and Helen could resolve to focus on their own collaboration and not make a presentation to their colleagues.
- The three teachers could delay their presentation and continue to discuss their different perspectives.
- The teachers could "agree to disagree" and each give her own perspective on their collaboration at the faculty meeting.
- The three teachers could solicit Kaye's input regarding a faculty presentation.

What implications might each possible next step have for Anita and her colleagues? How might it improve or worsen the situation?

4. Looking at the Bigger Picture. These questions can be used with the full group or with smaller groups.

Motivations and expectations for collegiality. Anita, Bibi, and Helen each had different reasons initially for seeking a collegial relationship. Anita wanted help with her LEP students; Bibi liked working with other teachers and wanted to pool ideas; Helen wanted to try working in a new way.

Do teachers have to share the same motivations and goals for a productive collegial relationship?

Do the motivations for collegiality have any influence on the nature or success of the collegial relationship?

Do all teachers (as well as administrators and parents) have to share the same kinds of expectations for collegiality in order to work together effectively? If not, how do those differences become assets and not liabilities in large-scale collaborations?

Nature of working collegially. Anita, Bibi, and Helen worked together by planning strategies that they all implemented in their classrooms.

Does a collegial relationship mean that teachers do the same things in their classrooms? Does it mean that they simply talk about what they already do in their classrooms? Does it mean that they create curriculum together? Does it mean that they define a common focus for their work together?

How extensive must the sharing and adoption of ideas, knowledge, and experience be for teachers to work collegially?

Anita, Bibi, and Helen had different personalities and different approaches to their work and to each other. This occasionally created some conflict or difficulties among them.

Are conflicts among small groups of colleagues inevitable?

How can conflicts be resolved in ways that preserve the collegial relationship?

Can collegial relationships benefit from conflict among colleagues? If so, how?

Scope and pace of changes that are driven by collegiality. Anita, Bibi, and Helen came to an agreement about what they wanted to work on together, although they had to negotiate the pace at which they effected changes in their classrooms.

When working collegially, to what extent is it important to reach agreement about the scope and pace of change?

How does working collegially affect the scope and pace of change attempted in schools?

Are the scope and pace of change related to the size of the group working together? Should a group of thirty, say, in comparison with a group of three, expect to spend much more time working together to bring about change? In what ways are comprehensive changes more possible with a large group? In what ways are they more challenging?

Role of collegiality in supporting and sustaining change. Anita might not have tried using parent volunteers and peer tutoring had she not collaborated with Bibi and Helen.

What are the benefits and problems of working collegially for a teacher's professional development and success in the classroom?

How does a collegial relationship foster successful change?

How does collegiality support and sustain change on a schoolwide scale? How is this different from (or similar to) collegial change on a smaller scale?

4

WHERE DO WE GO FROM HERE?

The Urban Mathematics Collaboratives (UMC), originally sponsored in part by the Ford Foundation, are initiatives in sixteen cities that seek to improve mathematics education in urban schools and to identify new models for meeting the professional development needs of mathematics teachers. Since their inception in 1985, the Collaboratives have provided opportunities for teachers to pursue innovative projects and engage in a range of leadership roles.

Education Development Center provided technical assistance to the Collaboratives, including teacher leadership workshops to help urban teachers think more broadly about school change while learning new skills and strategies to develop their own capacity for leadership. "Where Do We Go from Here?" was developed for use in these workshops to challenge participants to consider their roles as agents of change and as leaders in school reform efforts. The case recounts some of the challenges faced by a principal and teachers struggling to work creatively with categorical or specially designated funds to meet pressing school needs. The case offers opportunities to consider the nature of effective leadership by principals and by teachers.

The case is a fictionalized account of experiences described by Lavaun Dennett, former school principal and consultant on school restructuring. The authors express their appreciation to her for contributing to the development of this case. Funding for the development of the case was provided by the Ford Foundation as part of the UMC Technical Assistance and Outreach projects.

Characters

Helen Boulet, principal at Fairview Elementary

Rob Harkins, third-year first-grade teacher at Fairview Elementary

Diane Krupp, teacher with ten years of experience at Fairview Elementary

Joyce Washington, veteran fourth-grade teacher at Fairview Elementary

Sue Wong, librarian at Fairview Elementary

Manuel Ortiz, assistant superintendent of Oceanside Public Schools

Glossary

Chapter I. Federal legislation aimed at children from low-income families, providing schools with special funds to improve student achievement

THE CASE

Jessica Richter and Cynthia Lang

Helen looked again at the crayon drawings, maps, and stories displayed on the walls as she walked down the hallway toward the school's small library, where the faculty meetings were held. Except for the standard holiday-of-the-month bulletin board, these walls had been bare when she had arrived as the new principal of Fairview Elementary School. Now, three years later, they were covered with the green, yellow, and orange dinosaurs drawn by Ed Carvelli's third-grade science class. From the open classroom doors, Helen heard the sounds of students and teachers wrapping up the afternoon's lessons.

Around the corner came Rob Harkins, a third-year teacher in his mid-twenties, trailed by an excited group of fifteen first graders. As usual in his enthusiasm for his students' projects, Rob was late getting back to his classroom to get the kids ready to go home. As he walked the class past Helen, two of the children called to her in excitement. "We let them go, Ms. B!" "We opened the boxes and we read them our poems! They all flew away!"

For weeks Rob's first-grade class had been carefully tending their butterfly house as part of a science project, waiting and watching for the caterpillars to become cocoons and then colorful butterflies. On this May day, Helen knew, they had set their butterflies free, and each child had written a poem to celebrate.

"It must have been beautiful," said Helen, "I'd love to read all your poems. Will you bring them to me?"

As Rob and the students disappeared around the corner, Helen thought that her staff, too, had gone through a metamorphosis in their years together. It had been hard work, but they were finally beginning to form a real community that supported children's learning. So much has changed, Helen thought as she walked toward the faculty meeting, but where do we go from here?

Fairview Elementary

Helen remembered when she had walked down the hall to her first faculty meeting at Fairview three years ago. The bare walls had been covered with a peeling layer of schoolboard green paint. Behind closed doors, the muffled voices of teachers gave end-of-the-day directions. Outside one classroom, a sixth- or seventh-grade boy was standing by the wall casually enlarging a hole in the wall with a metal ruler.

Fairview Elementary School, when she arrived, was a small K–8 school (250 students) in Oceanside, a large western city. The Oceanside School District, the largest in the state, had been considered a system in trouble for several years. Superintendents remained in the district for an average of two years. Enrollment in the Oceanside Public Schools had continued to drop, even though Oceanside was one of the fastest growing metropolitan areas in the United States. Approximately 70 percent of Fairview's students were voluntarily bused to the school as part of the district's desegregation plan.

Some 25–30 percent of the students at Fairview were new to the school each year. One third of the students traditionally qualified for subsidized lunches, and half of the students lived in single-parent families. The school had averaged about 45–50 percent white, 45–50 percent African-American, and a scattering of other ethnic groups (5–7 percent) for about six years. Fairview historically categorized eighteen to twenty-two students a year (about 9 percent) as special education students. Historically, too, about one third of the staff turned over each year.

Helen had known from the beginning that her assignment as principal at Fairview would be a hard one. For one thing, it was only her second year in the role of principal. For another, she knew that the staff was wary of her alternative school background. They were used to authoritative leadership and tight, teacher-directed discipline. Helen believed that teachers should help students learn how to control themselves. In the first staff meeting, Helen remembered, she'd made matters even worse by emphasizing student self-control over teacher control. Teachers' positions had ranged from careful agreement to insistence that children would never be able to control themselves. The echoes in the hallways didn't die down for days. But Helen had been more convinced than ever that there was important work to be done at Fairview.

The Challenge

Helen saw from the beginning that the kids who were in trouble were the same kids who were always in trouble. More of the school's African-American students and students who qualified for subsidized lunches scored in the bottom ranges of standardized tests. And more of Fairview's special education students were African-American. It was the same pattern that others in education were talking about—kids were pulled out of their classrooms for special education, for Chapter I remedial education, and for special needs instruction, and still their scores weren't improving. To Helen, the problem was clear—tell kids they're broken, and they'll act like they're broken.

The easy part for Helen was knowing what needed to change at Fairview. Teachers needed to vary their instructional techniques and use more active, child-centered learning instead of lecturing or having kids work quietly alone. The hard part was convincing the staff to try some new ideas in their classrooms, and helping them see new possibilities for the school.

Experimenting with new teaching strategies was difficult for many of the teachers at Fairview. Giving up control in the classroom was a main concern. For some, like Diane Krupp, a teacher in her mid-thirties with ten years of classroom experience, having kids work in groups or do messy projects contradicted a teaching style that she had developed over the years. Diane's classroom was neat, organized, quiet, and disciplined. She believed that urban, low-income students needed limits set on their behavior and structured, quiet classrooms to balance their often disrupted home lives outside of school.

In staff meetings and in the faculty room, Diane took every opportunity to express her views, and she developed considerable support among the staff. At a staff meeting the day after a staff workshop on cooperative learning, Helen wasn't surprised when Diane spoke out.

"I suppose there were some good ideas in some of that group work," Diane began. "But what I don't see is how you break thirty-two kids into small groups and expect to keep any kind of order in the classroom or tabs on how the kids are doing. There are just too many students to be able to follow how the groups are working, and then help kids who are falling behind."

Helen was surprised at Joyce Washington's response. Joyce was a veteran teacher in her late forties with twenty-five years of experience as an elementary school teacher in the Oceanside schools. While Joyce was respected for her knowledge, patience, and experience, it was clear to most of the staff that she was tired of teaching. For about a year Joyce had been talking about getting out of teaching to work in a cousin's real estate firm, but so far she hadn't made any changes.

"I'm actually pretty excited about all this," commented Joyce. "There might be a lot of potential in trying some cooperative learning with our kids. I really think that I could have some fun putting my fourth graders in groups and requiring them to solve math problems together, say. It's not that trying cooperative learning isn't a good idea. But our large classes make it really difficult to try new things."

With Joyce's encouragement, a small group of teachers began to vary their instruction. As a group, they tried new ideas, and they began to work more closely as a team, collaborating on projects and giving each other feedback and ideas. Other teachers began to express interest in trying new classroom approaches. Helen responded by bringing consultants and teachers from other districts to Fairview to give professional development workshops, and she provided teachers with release time to attend classes and conferences.

Helen, believing that all decisions in the school should be made by the entire staff, called weekly (sometimes twice-weekly) staff meetings. These meetings became a forum where teachers could discuss their strategies and difficulties in the classroom, iron out differences, and challenge each other—and Helen—on schoolwide issues. More and more often, the Fairview teachers pointed to class size as a major barrier to trying new ideas in their classrooms.

Near the middle of her second year as principal at Fairview, Helen realized that real changes in classroom teaching weren't going to start happening at Fairview until they dealt with the issue of class size. Several teachers were using cooperative learning and doing some team teaching. Another group was just starting to try some new ideas. But most teachers were still wary of losing control or of losing track of student progress.

One weekend, Helen developed a scheduling plan for second semester. She announced it in a faculty meeting. "I have a new approach to scheduling that I would like to try for the rest of the year. I think this plan will help deal with some of the problems we've been discussing about class size, and will give us an opportunity to implement some new teaching ideas. For the rest of the year, I'd like to form cross-grade reading groups for one hour a day, with kids grouped by reading skill. We will pull all kids out of their classrooms and put every teacher in the building, including our Chapter I and special education teachers, in a classroom with a reading group. For one hour, we will really reduce class size."

Helen could feel weight shifting in the room. Someone rustled some papers. People made eye contact. Rob, then a second-year teacher who was jumping head-on into many of the new ideas, raised his hand. "Well, I think your plan seems like something to try," he said slowly. "I'd like to try it. What I'm wondering is, is this something we are definitely doing—that you want us to do—or are you asking for our feedback and ideas? It sort of sounds like you've made the decision by yourself."

Joyce Washington agreed. "It sounds worth trying, Helen, but I'd like to make sure that everyone is comfortable with this new idea and that we can give some input."

Helen started to tense, then smiled. She realized there had just been some kind of coup, but somehow she didn't seem to feel like the loser. "Okay. Perhaps I didn't approach this the best way. Does anyone have any ideas about where we might go from here?"

Promising Results

Over the next months, with staff input and involvement, Helen went ahead with the group's plan to form multi-age reading groups. In staff meetings, she encouraged the teachers to examine the structure of the school and to explore what worked and what needed to be changed. A small group of teachers decided to meet with Helen during the summer to plan an expanded program based on changes they had started at Fairview. Not everyone was happy with the changes. At the end of the year, five teachers asked to be transferred to different schools. New teachers, interested in Fairview's efforts, applied for open positions.

The plan, called the Fairview Program, began the following school year—Helen's third year as principal at Fairview. The goals for the program were to increase achievement for all students, eliminate labeling and pull-out programs, end teacher isolation, increase teacher effectiveness, and improve the achievement and behavior patterns of African-American students and students from low-income families. All students spent the morning in multi-age reading and mathematics groups, with no children labeled as Chapter I or special education students. The librarian, the science teacher, the Chapter I teacher, and the special education teacher all took reading and math classes, making it possible to reduce class size to 15 students. In the afternoon, students went back to their grade-level classes for social studies, science, and other subjects.

Helen continued to provide staff development, bringing in experts and practitioners with new ideas. In the process, some of the Fairview teachers became interested in specific subjects or teaching ideas and took advantage of opportunities to develop their own skills. Soon, they were giving workshops to their fellow teachers.

Concerned about meeting special education and Chapter I requirements, Helen met several times with Manuel Ortiz, Oceanside's assistant superintendent. Ortiz, who had experience as both a teacher and a principal, supported the changes at Fairview. His staff even helped Helen get a small grant from the Governor's School Improvement Initiative (see Figure 4.1). Helen remembered one particular phone call from Ortiz. "Helen, you and the Fairview teachers are beginning to do what few schools are succeeding at doing—improving the achievement of low-income and minority students. I really think you're getting at something important. If kids are learning more outside of their Chapter I and special education classes, then you're doing the right thing."

Helen and the teachers cultivated parent involvement. With Helen, a group of teachers organized a special night for parents to describe the Fairview Program and get parent input (see Figure 4.2). They brought people in from local community agencies at the same time, and made several follow-up calls to each child's home to encourage parents to attend. The whole staff was surprised and encouraged when almost 50 percent of the parents came to school for the event.

Fairview began to get more community attention. Helen invited visitors to the school. Two articles appeared in local papers, and Fairview was highlighted on one of the local news magazine shows. The Governor's office was following the Fairview Program closely through the School Improvement Initiative, and state legislators were beginning to point to Fairview as an example of the types of changes needed in urban schools.

But, amidst all the attention Fairview was getting, some teachers felt that Helen was pushing them too hard, too fast. Fairview teachers still had their share of students with serious discipline and learning problems, and many were still struggling to use new teaching strategies. Some staff members felt that efforts to draw attention to the Fairview Program were taking energy away from dealing with students. They complained about the issue among themselves, but no one had brought up the topic at a staff meeting.

One morning, while Helen was meeting with Sue Wong, the school librarian, Diane Krupp burst into her office, clearly upset. "Helen, this is too much! I haven't said anything up to now, but we need to get our priorities straight. I've had four visitors come into my reading class this morning alone. Every time someone walks in, the students get distracted and it takes five minutes to get them settled again. I'm all for people knowing about what we're doing here, but they're taking over the school!"

December 1, 1991

Dr. Manuel Ortiz
Assistant Superintendent
Oceanside School District
Building A
720 State Street
Oceanside, USA 90120

Dear Dr. Ortiz:

The Fairview staff and I would like to thank you for your assistance in securing a Governor's School Improvement Grant for Fairview Elementary School. These resources will provide valuable support in helping us to develop the Fairview Program to really meet the needs of all our students.

As you know, the Fairview Program is largely teacher-directed and initiated. All of the staff here are involved in every decision, and everyone is strongly committed to making the program work. I have attached a statement of Fairview's purpose/goals, which we developed together. I feel that articulating what we are trying to do is an important part of improving schools, and would be interested in your feedback.

Again, thank you for your assistance and support.

Sincerely,

Helen Boulet
Principal

FIGURE 4.1

Not quite sure what to say, Helen glanced at Sue. Bringing visitors to the school, she felt, was important to building support for the Fairview Program. But disrupting classes was unacceptable. How many other teachers felt the way Diane did? Helen responded slowly, "The last thing we want visitors to do is disrupt learning. But I think we do need to show people what we're doing here."

Sue agreed. "I think we want visitors, too, but they can sometimes be distracting. Maybe we should talk about all this in our next staff meeting, and try to make a schedule for visitors, or something."

At the next meeting, the staff decided to set aside certain days and times for school visitors, and agreed that teachers should know ahead of time when visitors would be in the school.

Although still struggling with new ideas, the staff was forming a cohesive team. Because teachers shared students during the day, they

The Fairview Program

Goals and Purpose

The Fairview Program is designed to increase achievement for all students, eliminate labeling and pull-out programs, end teacher isolation, increase teacher effectiveness, and turn around disproportionality patterns in the school. Disproportionality is a national pattern in which a disproportionate number of low-income and African-American students score in the bottom ranges of achievement tests, and have a greater tendency to drop out or become involved in disciplinary actions.

The Fairview Program focuses on around three primary themes:

1. <u>Reducing class size through more effective use of staff.</u> Pull-out classes have been eliminated, and all staff members are used to teach basic reading and mathematics skills in the morning. This flexible grouping provides ways to meet the diverse needs of students more effectively.

2. <u>Developing a comprehensive staff development program.</u> Staff receive regular training in areas such as Teacher Expectations/Student Achievement, Cooperative Learning, Learning Styles, Study Skills, Proactive Classroom Management, Active Participation, Whole Language Approach to Reading. Opportunities for peer coaching are available and encouraged.

3. <u>Restructuring the school day to better meet the needs of students.</u> Students are multi-age-grouped, curriculum is organized around integrated themes, and teachers have the flexibility to work in teams.

FIGURE 4.1 (Cont'd)

felt more responsible to the total school and worked more cooperatively. Said Joyce Washington in a news interview, "Everybody is just more at peace because of the smaller class sizes."

Diane Krupp echoed her feelings. "People aren't as stressed out. Teachers feel like their lessons are getting across to more children. And students are less frustrated."

As a group, the staff began to collect portfolios of student writing, and took attendance closely to monitor any changes or improvement. By April, Fairview students' scores on achievement tests had improved. The reading scores of African-American students improved eight percentile points, while those of other African-American students in the district at the same grade levels dropped six points. Scores for African-American students were up in math, too. African-American students at Fairview had scores an average of four points higher

October 17, 1991

Dear Parents,

YOU are a very important part of your child's education. We would like you to know how your child is doing in school, and want you to give us your ideas about how to make Fairview a better school.

Fairview Elementary School is starting a special program, called the Fairview Program, this year. The Fairview Program consists of many new ideas to help your son or daughter do better in school. Instead of staying in one classroom with one teacher all day, students at Fairview will be in reading and math groups during the morning and will go back to their regular classrooms in the afternoon. Children will get more attention from their teachers, because they will be in smaller classes. We want to talk with you about this plan and answer any questions.

Please come to the <u>Fairview Elementary School Parent Night on Tuesday, October 25, from 7 to 9:30 p.m. at the Fairview School, 135 Walnut St.</u> Your child's teachers will be at the school to talk with you about your son or daughter's progress, and about how you can help. People from other community organizations will also be at the school to answer questions you may have about childcare, health, employment, continuing education and training, and housing.

We hope you will come to Parent's Night. <u>If you have any questions or need a ride to the school, please call the school at 555-3337.</u> See you on October 25th!

Sincerely,

Fairview Teachers

Helen Boulet

Principal

FIGURE 4.2

than other African-Americans in the district. The staff was beginning to make further plans for changes for next year.

Today's Staff Meeting

Helen took a deep breath as she walked into the library. She wasn't sure how the staff was going to react to her announcement. At staff meetings lately, most of the news had been good. This wasn't. After about five minutes of general news and settling into the meeting, Helen spoke up. "I have a difficult announcement to make. As you know, the school district is facing a serious financial problem next year. They are talking about closing schools and laying off teachers. Yesterday, Manuel Ortiz at the superintendent's office called. He told me that, because we've stopped labeling Chapter I and special education students and have integrated them with other kids in our reading and math groups, the district has determined that Fairview won't be eligible for Chapter I or special education funding next year. This means that we may lose staff, or that we may have to redesign the program."

The room was silent for a moment. Then Diane called out from the back of room, "Well, that's just great. We do all this hard work, make all these changes, and it's just going nowhere. We all need our jobs."

"We have done a lot of hard work," said Rob, "and we're doing really good things at this school. There's got to be some other way to deal with this. Where do we go from here?"

FACILITATOR'S GUIDE

Deborah Bryant, Jessica Richter, and Cynthia Lang

This case is distinguished by the detailed chronology it provides of a school-based reform effort, and the opportunity it offers to consider issues of school leadership through analysis of its main character, elementary school principal Helen Boulet.

Synopsis of Case

Helen Boulet, an elementary school principal with alternative education experience, seeks to infuse a new vision into a traditional and troubled urban public school, Fairview Elementary School. Fairview is a small K–8 school of 250 students in Oceanside, a large western city. Over the past three years Helen has worked with her staff to restructure the school and establish a more innovative and effective model of education that will meet the needs of all the students. She also wants to reduce the tendency for minority and low-income students to be overrepresented in special education classes and labeled at-risk because of attendance and behavior problems.

Over three years Helen and the Fairview staff have begun to change the structure of the school, work more closely as a team, and involve members of the community and district administration. They have experimented with strategies to reduce class size and use categorical funds, like Chapter I and special education, in more creative ways. The case offers a detailed chronology of the development of the Fairview Program, an effort to increase student achievement by reducing class size, providing staff development for teachers, and restructuring the school day to better meet students' needs.

Helen and the staff manage to bring about some successes. As the case ends, however, they have just learned that the school now faces an unexpected and dismaying new challenge: funding cutbacks and potential loss of staff.

Major Issues

This case offers a chronology of events over a period of several years of a school reform effort. This chronology is useful for discussion of the following themes:

- Planning and carrying out a reform in school structure
- Optimizing staff involvement
- Promoting and building support for a new vision among parents, community, and school district
- Effective principal leadership for school reform efforts
- Teacher leadership for school change

Guiding the Discussion

We offer four suggested activities for building a discussion based on this case. We believe the sequence of the activities as presented offers a useful progression. However, the facilitator should tailor the format of the case discussion to the needs and interests of the participants, regarding the guidelines here as suggestions rather than as a script.

1. Focusing on the Issues is a whole group activity in which participants review the chronology of the case and identify the key issues it raises.
2. Understanding Principal Leadership is a small and large group activity in which participants analyze the principal's role in the case and extend the case to think more broadly about leadership.
3. Making Connections to Teacher Leadership is a small and large group activity in which participants analyze the teachers' roles in the case and reflect on their own leadership and the leadership of others in their own environment.
4. Considering Next Steps is an individual and large group activity addressing the final challenge presented in the case: the threat to the budget and staffing at Fairview Elementary.

1. Focusing on the Issues. This case has a more detailed chronology of events than some of the other cases in this book. This represents a challenge for facilitators and points to the need to spend some time at the beginning of the case discussion briefly reviewing the chronology and focusing participants on the larger issues raised by the events at Fairview Elementary.

Review the situation in the case to ensure that the group has a common understanding of the information presented before considering various issues, alternatives for action, and implications.

Can someone give a brief description of what has happened in the case?

Can someone else add to that description?

What is the problem from Helen's perspective? How does she feel about it?

What is the problem from the teachers' perspective? How do they feel about it?

What are the key issues raised by the case?

Push participants for a richer description of the underlying issues by encouraging them to give responses that go beyond the dramatic issue raised at the end of the case.

It is quite likely that the issues of Helen's leadership, her empowerment of the teachers, or her style of facilitating staff meetings will come up in the course of discussion. However, if they do not, you may want to raise them as issues yourself, as the next activity focuses on these aspects of the case.

2. Understanding Principal Leadership. In this activity, participants analyze the principal's role in the case and extend the case to think more broadly about leadership and change. This activity uses both small group and large group discussion formats.

Small group discussion. Ask participants to return to the case and underline text where they see examples of Helen in her role as principal acting as leader. Then, using this information, they should write a response to the question, What are the leadership challenges Helen faces? Each small group should generate a list of the challenges on flip chart paper or overhead transparency.

As small groups are working, walk around and observe. Encourage individuals to ground their analysis in the evidence in the case by asking questions such as, What does Helen do/say/think that is indicative of leadership in that example? What is the evidence in the case?

The lists groups generate begin to paint a picture of Helen as a leader and change agent. Ask each group to come up with a description of Helen's leadership style. (You can have fun with this by also asking them to choose a title or name for her that suits her leadership style. For example, Helen the Bold, or Helen the Gentle.)

Large group discussion. Have each small group briefly share a short description of the main leadership challenges they see Helen faced with and the words they would use to describe her as a leader. (Have them use the flip chart paper or transparency as a visual record of their conversation.)

Encourage conversation in the large group about the similarities and differences across the groups in their analysis of Helen's leadership.

In the case, Helen attempts to empower the teachers to participate in decision making at the school. The case says that Helen believed "that all decisions in the school should be made by the entire staff" and that "in staff meetings, she encouraged the teachers to examine the structure of the school and to explore what worked and what needed to be changed." Read these statements out loud to the groups and then, creating a large group discussion, ask,

Do you think that Helen practiced what she preached? How?

What do you think of her leadership style? What are its strengths? weaknesses?

What other leadership styles could Helen have adopted? What are their strengths and weaknesses?

These questions may prompt participants to offer opinions without corresponding evidence from the case. Good facilitative questions are, Where do you see that demonstrated? What is the evidence from the case that leads you to believe that?

3. Making Connections to Teacher Leadership. The style of leadership that Helen advocates calls for a change in role for teachers as well as for herself as principal. In fact, it requires teachers to be leaders in many respects, contributing to the development and implementation of a vision and a plan for school improvement. This activity uses a combination of small and large group discussion and individual reflection to focus on issues of teacher leadership raised by the case.

Small group discussion. Have each group choose a teacher (Diane, Joyce, or Rob) to focus on for this exercise. Ask participants to scan the text of the case one more time, noting examples of that teacher's role in the case. Ask them to discuss the following questions in small groups:

What are the concerns of this character in each section of the case? Specifically consider the concerns in the sections of the case titled The Challenge and Promising Results.

Do you consider this character a leader? Why, or why not? What is an example in the case of this person's leadership?

The case does not offer a lot of evidence of the characters' perspectives in the final section of the case, Today's Staff Meeting. In fact, it offers minimal data on Diane's and Rob's reactions and no data on Joyce's reaction. This is an opportunity for participants to extend the case based on their character analyses. Ask them to consider how the character they are discussing will respond to the dilemma at hand. What will this character's concerns be?

Large group discussion. Have each small group present its analysis of a character, by describing the character's concerns and whether the group believes the character is a leader. Encourage discussion by comparing and contrasting the profiles.

Individual reflection. Ask participants to write in response to the following reflective questions:

How would you define teacher leadership?

Would you characterize yourself as a teacher leader? Why, or why not?

Ask participants to share examples of definitions with the whole group. Record and discuss.

4. Considering Next Steps. This activity gives participants the opportunity, through the use of individual reflection and group discussion, to step into the shoes of Helen Boulet and the staff, and consider how they can use the forum of the staff meeting to address the current school district challenge.

Individual reflection. Ask participants to go beyond the story line of the case and to write responses to the following questions:

What is the problem the school now faces?

What is the leadership challenge?

As a staff, what should they do now? What would you do in a similar situation?

Large group discussion. After participants have had an opportunity to reflect on these questions individually and write down responses, ask them to share examples. A large group discussion of strategies will allow participants to hear, consider, and challenge others' ideas and extend their own. Prompt discussion with questions such as the following:

What would be the benefits of that approach? What would be the risks?

What are the implications of that approach for Helen as a leader? for the teachers as leaders?

5

ALMOST THERE—
OR ARE WE?

In 1990 the Michigan state legislature passed Public Act 25, a comprehensive education reform package. The legislation encouraged local school districts to reconsider what students needed to know, and know how to do, across the curriculum. The state offered a model set of core curriculum outcomes but encouraged districts to adapt these frameworks through a process of local school improvement planning. The Michigan Partnership for New Education, a joint venture of Michigan's public, private, and professional education sectors dedicated to transforming teaching and learning in the state's public schools and communities, directed its Educational Extension Service (EES) to support school districts in examining and implementing curriculum frameworks. The EES charted a process and created resource materials for local planning groups to use in developing curriculum frameworks.

Included in this set of resources was the case "Almost There—Or Are We?," developed by Education Development Center in collaboration with the EES. The case chronicles the progress of a local curriculum frameworks task force as it considers changes to the curriculum. The case supports participants in reflecting upon both the key issues that shape a curriculum and the process a local, school-based planning group might undertake to develop consensus on those key issues as it constructs a solid and thoughtful core curriculum.

"Almost There—Or Are We?" is an account of four meetings and an informal discussion of the fictional Lasker 2010 Task Force. The story line and discussions in the case are based on information provided by Michigan educators and on a core set of key curricular issues identified by the EES and its partners, although the dialogue, events, and exhibits were created specifically for this case. Funding for the development of the case was provided by the EES.

Characters

Greg Martin, owner of Martin Publishing Company
Donna Sanders, parent with three children in Lasker schools
Marian Scott, high school social studies teacher
Sylvia Chan, middle school principal
Bob Terris, high school math teacher and department chair
Judith Chavez, staff developer

THE CASE—PART I

Jennifer Nichols, Ilene Kantrov, Jan Ellis, and Cynthia Lang

Fourth Task Force Meeting, January 22

"It's amazing how much we've accomplished over the last three meetings," Greg Martin said, as he, Donna Sanders, and Marian Scott entered the committee room of Lasker's school department. They had arrived early for the fourth meeting of the 2010 Task Force. "What do you think, Marian? We've really been productive, huh?"

"Seems that way . . . ." Marian's voice trailed off as she sat down at the large conference table and began to unload papers from her briefcase. It was not the enthusiastic response Greg had anticipated. An awkward hush settled on the room.

Donna, just beginning to review the flip charts from the group's past three meetings, turned to Greg and said, "Well, I think we're on our way. Sure, we have some minor disagreements. But we can at least start a memo to the superintendent about how we see the issues—funding aside, since he encouraged us not to worry about that at this stage. And I'm really anxious for his input. Maybe I'm being naive, but I feel that once we pin down our priorities, it will make a big difference in our school system, and in the way we help kids prepare for the future."

Greg was pleased he at least had Donna's full attention. "I'm with you on that," he said as he glanced through his meeting notes. "Everything we've talked about—collaborative learning, higher-order thinking, alternative testing—I can see how these issues really affect how kids turn out. Times have changed. And we'd better change with them, or our kids are going to be left behind."

Marian finally looked up from her papers. "All this talk about change may sound fine to you," she said, shaking her head. "But you're not in the classroom day after day with thirty teenagers! Let me put it bluntly!" She slammed her pencil down on the table. "Lots of kids are lost as it is. They can't even remember the basic stuff, like math facts and vocabulary. Why, most of my high school juniors in American history don't even know the dates of the Civil War! There's so much we have to cover. And now everyone's excited about having kids carry out student-initiated investigations to answer some questions they think are interesting. When will they ever get the basics they really need? All I know is, in my history class, Richmond has to fall by October or we're in trouble!"

Background

The 2010 Task Force was organized in September 1990 at the request of Lasker's superintendent of schools, Dr. Albert Rossi (see Figure 5.1). Rossi asked a diverse group of educators, as well as a business executive and a parent, to examine ways in which the schools could better prepare students for the demands of the twenty-first century.

Among Lasker citizens, concerns about the schools' inability to supply skilled graduates to meet the demands of the workplace had been brewing for some time. A rash of letters to the editor of the Lasker *Star-Tribune* expressed the fears of some in the community that the city was headed for inevitable decline. According to rumors, one long-time company was even threatening to hire workers from Finland!

This was not the first time that Lasker citizens had been troubled by the threat of economic decline. The city had been on a gradual downslide since the closing of Lasker Steel Corporation, the area's major provider of unskilled, high-paying jobs. A brief glimmer of recovery occurred in the 1970s, when a group of community leaders revitalized the old steel plant and turned it into an attractive complex of office space, shops, and restaurants. But even this development hadn't attracted the stable, diversified business base needed to inject new life into the city of 55,000. Linked to these economic troubles were increasing social problems, particularly among young people: higher dropout rates, absenteeism, teenage pregnancy, and alcohol and drug use.

Fourth Task Force Meeting, January 22 (Cont'd.): Looking Back

Waiting for the others to arrive, Donna Sanders returned to the flip charts and reviewed the group's discussions in the first three meetings.

First Task Force Meeting, September 25. The first chart, compiled by Greg Martin, summarized the gap between entry-level require-

LASKER CHAMBER OF COMMERCE

August 10, 1990

Dr. Albert Rossi
Superintendent
Lasker Public Schools
1518 N. Maple St.
Lasker, MI 40000

Dear Al:

I am very pleased that you have decided to form a task force to address the concerns the business community shares with others in Lasker about the preparation of our young people for living and working in the 21st century. As I mentioned on the phone the other day, in the past few months two companies that were considering moving into the new industrial park on Route 25 decided not to site their plants here. When Greg Martin of Martin Publishing called the presidents of these companies to find out what factors tipped their decisions against Lasker, both stressed their doubts about the schools. One of them, who runs Midwest Direct Mail, which is looking to relocate, said outright, "We just didn't think the Lasker schools were going to be able to supply the kinds of people we'll need over the next ten to fifteen years."

The direct mail business is a high-tech operation. Midwest will be hiring people to do everything from running and repairing data-processing equipment to word processing, proofreading, graphic design, sales, marketing, and accounting. Nearly everything there is computerized—list processing, sales projections, scheduling, billing, payroll. And things change fast in the business. Every couple of years their whole way of operating can be revolutionized by a new piece of software or even a whole new technology. They need people who are flexible, who have really good math and communication skills, who are willing and able to learn new, complex ways of doing things, who apply themselves to their work, and who can work together well to complete a job.

The other company, Select Plastics, is planning to move its company headquarters and build a new production plant. Select recently considered relocating its plant overseas to reduce costs. Instead they've decided to reorganize the way they operate in order to cut down on indirect costs—inspections, repairs, maintenance, scheduling, supervision—everything over and above direct production expenses. The new plant is going to eliminate many of the low-skill, low-paying jobs. The remaining employees will work in teams responsible for increasing efficiency and productivity. They will need to be able to maintain machinery, plan production, troubleshoot equipment problems, use computers, and monitor quality.

With this reorganization, the qualifications of entering employees will be critical. The president was worried that Select would have to invest too much in providing remedial help to new employees here before they could even receive the training the company itself will provide. He also said that some of the managers of his company who learned of the possible move were concerned about sending their own kids to our schools. One of their top vice presidents even threatened to quit her job before she'd send her kids to school here!

The message seems pretty clear. If we're going to be able to fill up that industrial park and keep on attracting other businesses, we need to do something

FIGURE 5.1

about the way our schools prepare kids for the workforce. All of us at the Chamber of Commerce are therefore delighted with your initiative. Greg has volunteered to serve as the business representative on the task force, and he looks forward to working with the other members to figure out how we can make our schools and graduates more competitive.

Sincerely,

Carl Williams
President

P.S. If you and the members of the task force would like some background on the changing needs of business as we head into the 21st century, I've just had a look at two reports that make compelling reading. They are *America's Choice: High Skills or Low Wages!* (Rochester, NY: National Center on Education and the Economy, 1990, especially pages 19–38) and *Workforce 2000: Work and Workers for the 21st Century* (Indianapolis: Hudson Institute, 1987). You might also want to consider the graph I've attached, which is from another report, *The Business Roundtable Participation Guide: A Primer for Business on Education* (New York: National Alliance of Business). It compares the actual skill levels of new workers with the skill levels needed for new jobs.

cc: Greg Martin

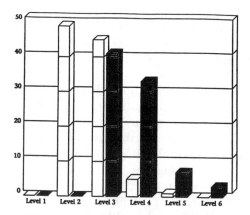

☐ Actual Skill Levels of New Workers (Skill levels of current 21–25 year olds)
■ Skill Levels Needed for New Jobs (Skill levels of net new jobs being added to the economy between 1985 and 2000)

Level 1   Has limited reading vocabulary of 2,500 words. Reading rate of 95 to 125 words per minute. Ability to write simple sentences.
Level 2   Has reading vocabulary of 5,000 to 6,000 words. Reading rate of 95 to 215 words per minute. Ability to write compound sentences.
Level 3   Can read safety rules and equipment instructions, and write simple reports.
Level 4   Can read journals and manuals, and write business letters and reports.
Level 5   Can read scientific/technical journals and financial reports, and write journal articles and speeches.
Level 6   Has same skills as Level 5, but more advanced.

Source: Hudson Institute, *Preparing Workforce 2000.* Reprinted in *The Business Roundtable Participation Guide: A Primer for Business on Education* (New York: National Alliance of Business).

FIGURE 5.1 (Cont'd)

ments in Greg's printing company and the work behavior of many young people he had hired over the past few years:

ENTRY-LEVEL COMPANY NEEDS	ENTRY-LEVEL WORKERS' BEHAVIOR
Motivation	Many unmotivated and uninterested
Concentration	Unable to focus; inattentive
Teamwork	Not team players; trouble with co-workers and supervisors
Communication	Poor writing and speaking skills
Problem solving	Lack initiative, creativity, ability to carry out complicated procedures
Vision	Can't see how their job contributes to final product

As Greg had finished jotting down the final point on the chart, he had said, "Kids nowadays don't realize that what they do, or don't do, can affect the success of the whole job. In my business, everyone's task depends on the previous process being done correctly. There's no doubt about it." He'd firmly underscored the word *teamwork* on the chart. "Today's jobs require a high level of teamwork—we're not talking isolated factory tasks anymore. And I can guarantee that every other CEO in town agrees with me!"

The group, sympathetic to Greg's frustrations, had nodded in agreement as he spoke. "Can you give us an example, Greg?" Sylvia Chan had asked. "Something from your company?"

"Sure," Greg had answered. "I won't forget this one—almost cost me a major client. Last month, I hired a high school grad to train with one of my older employees on desktop publishing. We had a rush catalogue job, and the trainer gave a portion to this kid, thinking he could handle it. Well, he couldn't. But instead of asking for help, the kid fiddled around with the machine and botched the job. At the last minute, the older guy rushed to redo it and ended up revising the wrong original, putting in wrong pricing information. And it went to press that way! It was breakdown all along the line. This kid wouldn't ask for help and couldn't adapt what he had learned in school to this new situation. And the worst part was, when the problem surfaced, instead of getting together to figure out how to deal with it, they both blamed each other for what had gone wrong."

"What Greg says is true," Sylvia had agreed. "Sometimes, I think that those of us who work in schools feel so isolated that we forget that elsewhere people are constantly relying on each other."

"And," Greg had interrupted, "that can mean the person next to them, or someone halfway around the world. In some businesses, employees communicate via satellites and telecommunications, and depend on people they'll never meet."

"That's right. But you have to admit," Bob Terris had added, "that most classrooms are set up to teach kids to keep their eyes on their own work and to get ahead at the expense of other kids." He had glanced back at the flip chart. "No wonder so many of them fit Greg's description!"

"What always bothered me in school," Donna had said, "was that there were only so many A's that could be given out. Somebody always had to fail. And you got in trouble if you asked someone else for help with your work. I even see this with my own children. How can we teach kids to cooperate?"

"I don't think you 'teach' them," Sylvia had responded. "You set the context for cooperation to happen."

"What do you mean?" Greg had asked.

"Well, the most exciting example that comes to mind was reported last spring in the Schools section of the *Star-Tribune*. Remember the article? It was about the three teachers from Worthen Middle School who planned that terrific interdisciplinary unit about the history of the old Lasker Steel plant." (See Figure 5.2.)

"Yes, I read that, and it really struck me," Donna had responded. "It was so different from most of the things I did in school, which never seemed to have anything to do with life outside of school. What a fabulous project! Don't you think so?" she had asked as she turned to Judith Chavez.

"Absolutely!" Judith had agreed. "Those kids got to work on something extremely meaningful. I was involved in a small way—I helped the teachers round up resources, so I got to see the 'behind the scenes' planning. Believe me, it wasn't easy for those teachers. Each of them had to give up something to make the project work, and they had to negotiate all kinds of turf issues. But it was a great opportunity for collaboration at all levels—in the town, within the school, among the teachers—and most important—among students."

Marian had looked doubtful. "I can see how that would work in the middle schools, where the curriculum isn't as fixed, and where teachers have more flexibility. But in the high school, each subject has a set syllabus, and we simply cannot take time out to do something that's not in the syllabus."

"Well, but isn't that exactly the point?" Greg had asked, barely giving Marian a chance to finish speaking. "In business, Marian, if we

Worthen students contribute to Lasker's History

By Cassandra Warner
STAR-TRIBUNE STAFF

As Worthen Middle School eighth graders stroll through the Lasker Steel Complex and its surrounding area, they can see beyond the trendy restaurants, inviting shops, and renovated townhouses that now occupy Lasker's once-thriving steel plant. "I think about those kids our age who used to work all day in that plant," said Joseph Haddad, 13. "I try to imagine how hot it must have been in the foundry," said Amy Liu, 14. Russ Gibb, 13, explained, "In some ways, life wasn't so bad back then. People got together a lot and had fairs, dances, and all sorts of contests."

How did these students learn about Lasker's past? For two months, they have been researching the last 100 years of the Lasker Steel Complex and its surrounding neighborhood. Using public records and photographs, biographical journals, and personal interviews with elderly Lasker residents, the young researchers have pieced together a rich and intriguing history of the Lasker plant's neighborhood.

The project, entitled "Lasker 100," was the brainchild of three Worthen teachers: Tina Johnson, a language arts teacher, Lynn Bourque, a social studies teacher, and math teacher Lou Ortiz. "We wanted the students to approach research in a different, more exciting way," said Bourque. "By letting kids' interests and inquiries about the Lasker plant determine their topics, we hoped that research would become more meaningful and personal to students."

Were their expectations met? "You bet," said Johnson. "I've never seen kids so involved and excited about a project in all my years of teaching!"

One goal of the three teachers, each representing different subject areas, was to plan a unit that would provide students with an exciting interdisciplinary learning experience. The group developed the "Lasker 100" unit during the fall and winter; by March they were ready to try it out in their classrooms.

"The unit required tremendous teamwork," said Ortiz, "and support from all levels of the school district was essential. Our principal, the superintendent, and the district's math, language arts, and social studies consultants were all involved in some way."

Teamwork was required not only of the teachers, but of the students as well. Student research teams of three or four collaborated on researching, writing, and producing a final report. "Kids really had to learn to work together," explained Johnson, "and believe me, it wasn't a piece of cake for everyone. There was lots of negotiating, compromising, communicating, and even some complaining that went on. But kids learned an important lesson: how to stick with a task and work it out with others."

Explained Fred Nassif, 13, coauthor with two other students of "One Day in the Life of a Child Laborer," "It was really fun! We all got into the topic, we helped each other find information, and we worked on the report together. We even did illustrations for it on the computer."

Vicki Shaw, 14, was especially excited about her group's report on schooling. "I talked to my grandparents about what it was like when they went to school. I couldn't believe some of the things they told me—like the teachers used to hit kids' knuckles with a ruler if they talked to each other in class!" Shaw's group reported not only on methods of punishment but also the kinds of textbooks students used and what they were expected to learn. With math teacher Ortiz's help, the Worthen researchers also used old enrollment records to figure out how few of the students fifty years ago went past the eighth grade.

FIGURE 5.2

In all, over forty Lasker senior citizens were interviewed for the project. Students questioned them about changes in employment, housing, customs, entertainment, leisure time, education, and cost of living. Several students even reported receiving gentle advice during the interview. According to Jason Harmon, 14, Al Lopez, 78, told him to "study hard, keep your hair short, and stay in school."

At the conclusion of the research, each group of students wrote up their findings in a report. "The format of the report was mostly up to the students," stated social studies teacher Bourque. In reporting their information, the majority used three main headings: "What we wanted to find out and why," "What we found out and how," and "What we learned." Johnson, the language arts teacher, stressed that the reports did not just "flow" from students' pens. "Kids went through a writing process," she explained. "They generated lots of ideas, wrote and rewrote several times, then edited before arriving at a final product."

The final product represented the collaborative efforts of each research team. Explained Ortiz, "Each report was bound as a hardcover book and presented in a special ceremony to the Lasker Historical Society. The society staff was incredible. We gave them the report titles prior to the ceremony, and by the time we arrived they had already catalogued the reports in their permanent records, which the class viewed on the computer. The kids were so proud that their reports were part of such an important collection."

Jane Alvino, president of the society, said, "This represents a truly significant contribution to our city's history. Worthen students uncovered many interesting facts—some unknown even to us! I hope this is the first of many school-community projects, and I invite anyone interested to browse through the reports in the society's collection."

What's the next challenge for the teachers and students of Worthen? Student Brian Sachs, 13, offered this suggestion: "Maybe we can research the history of the whole state and then give our reports to the governor!"

Teachers who want to know more about the "Lasker 100" project may attend a series of workshops to be given by the Worthen teaching team. For information, contact Tina Johnson at the Worthen Middle School, 30 Webster Ave., Lasker MI 40000; telephone 555-3579.

FIGURE 5.2 (Cont'd)

have a plan that's not working, we have to make some changes. And if what's in the current 'business plan' for the schools isn't producing students with the sorts of skills we need, then don't we need to change the plan?"

Second Task Force Meeting, October 23. At the second meeting, Bob had volunteered to keep notes on the flip chart. It had been easy to summarize the information from the first part of the discussion, when group members had brainstormed the terms they associated with higher-order thinking skills versus the basics:

HIGHER-ORDER THINKING SKILLS	BASICS
Analyzing	Math facts
Drawing inferences	Grammar
Solving problems	Vocabulary
Creating	Phonics

This straightforward discussion was short-lived, however. Judith's comment had set off a heated debate: "In the past twenty-five years," she had said, eyeing the Basics column on the flip chart, "curricula and textbooks have been spoonfeeding kids and not challenging them to do any thinking on their own. They learn fact after isolated fact, and never have the opportunity to apply what they learn in a meaningful way."

"But didn't we get by okay?" Donna had asked. "I admit that textbooks weren't exactly fascinating reading. But I did learn from them, and I remember how proud I was when I mastered something—like dates of important events, or names of significant battles."

"No offense, Donna," Judith had countered, "but it's not a matter of parroting what a textbook, or even a teacher, tells us. If we're talking about preparing kids to function in the real world, then they've got to experience situations where their own brainpower gets them to a solution."

"We're not denying that the basics are the fundamentals on which we build education," Bob had agreed, "but even these basics are changing—advancing right along with our society. We've got to help kids cope with today's complex world, and that means helping them learn how to think out a problem and how to learn what they don't know. Our hope is that all kids will be enthusiastic, lifelong learners. When will we acknowledge that what is basic to kids today vastly exceeds the three R's?"

"I question that," Marian had interjected, her face flushed. "My thirty years as an educator in this system have convinced me of the need for good, strong, basic education. If you can read, write, and calculate, you can learn whatever you need, from computer programming to aeronautical engineering. Surely you've read *Why Johnny Can't Read* and *Crisis in Education*?" she had said as she surveyed each group member. "We've got to commit ourselves to stricter discipline and to teaching traditional subjects—the type of education that got all of us where we are today. How can we possibly expect students to function at these higher levels if they can't even master the basics?" she had asked. "I'm just not convinced!"

"I know that the basics have always shaped our educational system, Marian," Sylvia had said. "And Judith, I agree about the need for higher levels of thinking. But I have my own dilemma as an administrator. When I supervise a teacher, I look for instruction that's alive, that excites and challenges students. I don't want to see kids at their desks filling out worksheets. And the best classes seem to be the ones where students really care about what they're doing, so they're willing to work hard."

"Right. That's just what happened in the Lasker 100 project," Judith had added. "Students' questions guided their research and held their interest throughout the project."

"I know," Sylvia had agreed. "When I'm in a classroom like that, I feel as though there's real learning going on. But then I have a problem: We have a scope and sequence in each subject that each teacher is responsible for. If students' curiosity determines the direction of the class, then how do we develop a reasonable scope and sequence, and how do the teachers stick to it? How do they assure that the class covers all the material in that scope and sequence? Do you see my dilemma?" Bob, returning to the flip chart he had started at the beginning of the meeting, had made several attempts to summarize the discussion. Finally, he had turned to the group for help. "I'm having a hard time capturing all of the points we've discussed. Any ideas?"

Third Task Force Meeting, November 27. "One thing has been bothering me," Donna had said as the group began their third meeting on November 27. "I think it's related to the dilemma Sylvia was talking about at the last meeting. If kids are spending their time on the kinds of projects we've been talking about, like the Lasker 100 project at the Worthen school, then what about their test scores? I know how important these are. My sister, who's a real estate agent, carries around the test scores of every school in the district!"

"You're right, Donna, it's incredible how test scores are used and misinterpreted—by everyone," Sylvia had answered. "I'm held accountable for the success of my school, and that's measured by test scores. You should hear the complaints when those scores go down."

"In math," Bob had added, "we're starting to recognize that many of these tests don't measure a lot of what we need to be teaching. The National Council of Teachers of Mathematics has recently come out with new standards for math education, and my department has really been struggling to think about how our own testing, as well as what we teach, may need to shift."

"But one good thing about the tests we have," Marian had offered, "is they're objective. You know where kids stand. And they don't take hours and hours of our time to score. There was a time when I used to give essay questions. But I got more and more arguments from kids about how I was grading them. And the writing was just atrocious. I found I was spending so much time correcting their grammar that I never got to teach history. It just wasn't worth it."

"You know, testing is a problem, but we're not the only ones facing it," Judith had contended. "It's a nationwide issue. Many state boards of education are developing new methods of measuring what students can do. They're looking at using student projects and portfolios and focusing more on evaluating thinking skills, such as problem solving, and applying knowledge to real-world problems. With this type of assessment, kids have a chance to master real bodies of knowledge and to integrate different subject areas in a meaningful way."

"Yes, that's the direction we need to move in," Bob had agreed. "There's got to be a better way. I recently heard about an entire school that spends weeks preparing kids for one standardized test—you know, priming them on how to fill in the blanks, giving them lots of practice answering multiple-choice questions, urging them to get a good night's sleep and to eat a good breakfast, and so on."

"No wonder my kids are basket cases before one of those tests!" Donna had exclaimed.

"Right—just imagine the anxiety level on the 'big day,'" Bob had agreed. "But in the end, these tests don't tell us a whole lot that's of use."

"Well, they do tell how well kids can recognize the right answer out of a predetermined list of responses!" Judith had announced. "And how well they've been coached on picking out grammar and punctuation errors in a passage. But they don't tell us how kids can solve problems, consider and evaluate alternatives, or synthesize and interpret information—the skills they desperately need for the future. Believe me, what you test is what you get. And I'm afraid that the tests we put so much trust in are not giving us what we need!"

Fourth Task Force Meeting, January 22 (Cont'd.)

Donna folded back the last flip chart just as Judith, Sylvia, and Bob entered the room.

"Sorry we're late, everyone," Judith began. "Since we're all here now, does everyone feel comfortable about writing a memo to the superintendent? I know we're not in total agreement about how we want to present the issues, but at least we know what the issues are, and . . ."

"Wait a minute," Greg interrupted. "We've just been talking, and Marian raised some questions that I think we'd better work on some more before we make any decisions. Marian?"

"Well, I've really mulled this over a lot, Judith," Marian began slowly. "I hope you don't think I have a closed mind. I understand that the world is changing, that kids growing up today face a different future from kids thirty years ago, when I started teaching. But the way we've been framing the issues takes us in a direction that I find troubling. Like the middle school research project we talked about and some of the higher-order skills we've been saying are important: I do get excited about those sorts of things for the students who are high achievers. But what about the kids who won't be going to college? Believe me, some of these ideas are only for a chosen few—the cream of the crop. For the rest, well, we just can't afford to take time away from teaching the basics."

Study Questions

1. What is this case about? How would you summarize it?
2. What are the key curricular issues that the Lasker 2010 Task Force is addressing?
3. What important curricular issues is the task force failing to identify and consider?
4. What could you draw on from your own experience that could help the members of the task force in their discussion of the issues when they meet with the superintendent?

THE CASE—PART II

Jennifer Nichols, Ilene Kantrov, Jan Ellis, and Cynthia Lang

"Something's really been nagging at me lately," Sylvia said as she, Greg, and Donna met in Greg's office several days after the fourth meeting of the 2010 Task Force to review some community outreach materials. "You know, all through our discussions, we've been so focused on preparing kids for the workplace. What about preparing them for citizenship? Wasn't that the original goal of education? And isn't it more important?"

Greg looked annoyed. "The way things are shaping up, we'd better put all our energies into preparing kids for work, or we'll really be in trouble!"

"Before you two get carried away . . . ," Donna interrupted, as she set aside a stack of papers. "I'm not sure what you're actually talking about, Sylvia."

"Well, let me back up, and tell you what started me thinking about this." Sylvia took a folder from her briefcase and handed it to Greg and Donna. "Glance at this proposal. I reviewed it a few days ago—it's from a high school social studies teacher who's requesting funds to take a group of juniors to a student conference on state government at the capital." (See Figure 5.3.)

When Greg and Donna finished reading, Sylvia continued. "At first, I was really excited about our kids having these opportunities—student forums, actual legislative work, teleconferences. I thought that the long-term impact of this project would be great for the kids and the whole community."

"I really don't see the point of this, Sylvia," Greg said as he pushed the proposal aside. "How many kids are going to run for office? Why send them off to the capital? Kids need preparation for real jobs!"

**LASKER PUBIC SCHOOLS
MINI-GRANT PROPOSAL**

NAME: Laurie Plaut

SCHOOL: Lasker High School

TITLE: Community Participation: Spotlight on Citizenship

PROJECT DESCRIPTION
Phase I — Spotlight on Citizenship

I would like to take my eleventh-grade social studies class to the state capital to participate in "Spotlight on Citizenship," a three-day student conference that promotes understanding of our state government and active participation in the democratic process. Student activities will include student-led forums, meetings with journalists and political figures, and problem-solving sessions. Students will also participate in teleconferences in which citizens from across the state discuss issues with government officials.

There are two major goals of this year's conference: (1) to promote student interaction with decision makers, and (2) to identify issues of concern in our state that are relevant to teenagers. Students will work with a legislator for one day to identify a current issue of teen concern in the state, and learn ways of collecting related information, communicating with constituents, informing the public, and proposing action.

Phase II — Making a Difference

Back in the classroom, students will work in groups to identify a meaningful community problem in Lasker (for example, youth crime, environmental problems, drug abuse, public safety, homelessness). Related activities will include collecting information about the problem, gaining input from community members, and developing a plan of action that can make a difference (for example, letter-writing campaigns, petitions, public meetings, educational materials, cable TV spots, contacting local businesses, enlisting volunteers). Project culmination will be a forum at which students discuss their issues and answer questions about their action plans in front of an audience of peers and invited adults.

Phase III — Community Service

Next year, incoming juniors will participate in the final component of the project: community service. After attending the "Spotlight on Citizenship" conference (Phase I) and identifying a problem in Lasker (Phase II), students will work with a community organization to develop and implement their plans of action. For example, a group of students whose issue is homeless youth could work with the Department of Parks and Recreation to develop plans for a sports program

FIGURE 5.3

aimed at homeless children. The students might even enlist high school volunteers to work in the program, thus extending community service opportunities to others. Students will analyze, over the school year, the effects of their action plans.

BACKGROUND

Participatory citizenship, the foundation of a democracy, should be the focal point of social studies. Our current curriculum, however, fails to educate students to be active participants in a democratic society. Nationwide, this failing is underlined by the current crises in civic life—crime, drug abuse, public safety—and the failure of most citizens to grapple with these problems. We must help students develop into active, empathetic citizens who establish lasting links with our community, have a stake in the success of community institutions, and can take pride in their ability to truly "make a difference."

Literature on participatory citizenship suggests three important areas of need for curriculum improvement:

Knowledge. Students need in-depth knowledge about their own government and democracy as well as comparative knowledge about other forms of government to deepen their understanding of our democratic process.

Civic Environment. Students must be encouraged to act as responsible and responsive members of a community by actively grappling with civic problems.

Participation. Students should partake in honest, open talk about public problems. A democratic community can survive only with sustained dialogue about public problems. (Students need only to be reminded of the effects of glasnost in Russia to understand the impact of open, free talk.) Participation also includes opportunities to engage in community service.

MAJOR STUDENT GOALS

To acquire knowledge about how local decision making works.
To collect and interpret information on issues of public concern.
To work cooperatively with others.
To understand individual and group responsibility.
To actively and effectively communicate with others.
To listen to others' points of view and appreciate diversity.
To think critically about how to solve problems.
To act responsibly.

FIGURE 5.3 (Cont'd)

"Greg, look on the last page of this proposal—where the teacher lists her goals," Donna said. "It looks to me as if they're very similar to the goals we discussed for preparing kids for the workplace. Why don't we let Sylvia finish?"

"Well, as I was deciding how to respond to this proposal," Sylvia continued, "I started to think about our curriculum. And I realized that the courses we offer barely begin to prepare kids for 'participatory citizenship' as this teacher describes it. We're light years away! Civics, world history, western civ . . ."

"But we all took those courses." This time it was Donna who interrupted. "Sure, we're not holding public office—but we know what's going on in our community. We read the paper and we watch Ted Koppel. And our kids don't do so poorly, either. Remember that 'College Bowl' on current events with Jefferson High last year? Our kids were terrific! They knew all sorts of things—capitals, political figures, even geography."

"It's important to know those things," Sylvia agreed, "but does that type of knowledge really translate into political judgment? I mean, if the point is to get students to vote once in a while and to watch the nightly news, then what we have now is fine. But if kids are going to get involved in what's talked about in this proposal—real dialogue about public problems, informed decision making, community participation—well, that's another issue entirely."

"What do you mean by community participation, anyway?" Greg demanded as he sat back in his chair, folding his arms across his chest.

"It's helping kids understand citizenship and actually contribute to their communities in meaningful ways," Sylvia replied. "I mean, how many kids are aware of their responsibility for being part of the solution to problems that affect not only them, but their fellow citizens as well? Things like the environment, the homeless population, illiteracy, drug abuse. . . . When do kids have the chance and the encouragement to figure out how they can have an impact on these issues—make a difference? Most focus on meeting their own individual needs—deciding what to wear to the next dance, buying the next computer game."

"Is that all bad?" Donna asked. "The self-centeredness bothers me, too. But teenagers are at that stage where they need time to figure out who they are as individuals. I thought that part of the aim of education is to develop the whole person—someone who's well-rounded, creative, and intellectually curious. Personally, I want my kids to have a passionate interest in life and an awareness of art and beauty—for their own benefit."

"I agree that we should help kids be self-fulfilled," Sylvia said. "But meeting individual needs shouldn't exclude the needs of the community. Why, how many of our kids perform any type of community service?"

"Well, some high school kids volunteer at the hospital, and I know a few who help tutor at the elementary school," Donna offered.

"But," Sylvia countered, "I'll bet that none of them makes any connection between those experiences and what they learn in school."

Greg, tapping his pencil, spoke directly to Sylvia. "You can't expect to make everything part of schooling! First, you want to create junior politicians, and now you want to turn kids into social workers and missionaries. Marian was right—there's only so much class time! If teachers spend big chunks of it on community participation, what happens to the workplace skills?"

Study Questions

1. What is Sylvia's concern about the previous discussions of the task force? Can you summarize her argument?
2. How would you answer the question Greg poses to Sylvia at the end of their discussion?
3. After reading Part II, would you want to add to or change your list of key curricular issues? Why, or why not?

FACILITATOR'S GUIDE

Jennifer Nichols, Barbara Miller, and Ilene Kantrov

This guide is for the facilitator to use with educators, parents, and other community members who are engaged in the task of curriculum reform. Its purpose is to provide structure for this complex process and to bring out the major issues curriculum reform raises.

Synopsis of Case

"Almost There—Or Are We?" is an account of four meetings and an informal discussion of the Lasker 2010 Task Force. The task force is a diverse group of educators and community members charged with considering how their city's school system can better equip students for the challenges of the twenty-first century. Lasker, a small city of 55,000, has recently been shaken by the closing of its largest employer, Lasker Steel Corporation, and the community has directed its concern to the school system by questioning its ability to prepare students for the workplace of the future.

Part I opens as the task force convenes its fourth meeting. The group is planning to write a report to the superintendent summarizing the issues discussed and the progress made in the previous three meetings. As the meeting unfolds, however, the task force members realize that they are not in agreement; many key issues remain unresolved and even troubling to some members of the group.

Part II extends the case by including a conversation among several task force members about the connections between school and the world of work, and the implications for preparing students for citizenship.

Major Issues

This case situates discussion about curriculum reform in the context of seven key educational issues. These powerful issues pervade school life and underlie important decisions about the design, adoption, and implementation of a core curriculum. Embedded in all curricular areas, these issues are significant to the many constituencies involved in curriculum reform: teachers, parents, communities, and students.

Consideration of the issues, stated here as either-or propositions, does not involve trading one for the other or debating their relative merits. Rather, it is meant to provoke discussion about the underlying assumptions that shape people's opinions and influence their actions in moving toward curriculum reform. The issues are

1. Excellence versus equity
2. Depth versus breadth
3. Higher-order thinking versus basics
4. Real-world learning versus school learning
5. Learning community versus isolation and competition
6. Disciplinary versus interdisciplinary
7. Testing what you teach versus teaching what you test

Purpose of the Case

Through thoughtful and systematic discussion, participants can

- Work toward building personal understanding and elaborating their own ideas about important educational issues
- Appreciate and consider the views of the many constituencies involved in school change efforts
- Begin a process of building consensus around key issues by identifying and examining shared values

Guiding the Discussion

Although we provide some suggestions for discussion format (personal reflection, small and large group discussion), facilitators should tailor the format to the needs and interests of participants.

The questions, intended to be a guide rather than a script, are designed to build participants' understanding of the case and its issues through five discussion areas:

1. Focusing on the Issues
2. Examining Underlying Assumptions
3. Building Consensus
4. Articulating a Vision
5. Taking a Second Look

Note that this case is presented in two parts. We suggest that participants read and discuss Part I before considering Part II. The study questions at the end of Parts I and II of the case are intended to prompt reflection. Many of them are represented in the following activities.

1. Focusing on the Issues. Discussion in this section encourages participants to describe the case, identify key issues it raises, and focus their thinking on one set of issues.

Begin by asking participants,

What is the case about?

What key educational issues can you identify in this case?

The case developers intentionally included the seven issues listed previously (excellence versus equity, depth versus breadth, and so on). Participants may find other issues to add to the list or may frame the given issues in different terms.

Ask participants, working in small groups, to select one set of issues and develop a matrix of supporting evidence showing each task force member's perspective on that set of issues (see, for example, Figure 5.4). Ask each group to discuss and compare its matrix with those of other groups and, if it wishes, to revise its ideas. Encourage participants to identify other issues that are not addressed in this case, but should be, and add them to the matrix.

2. Examining Underlying Assumptions. Assumptions are beliefs that people hold to be true, based on their personal experiences. Con-

Higher-Order Thinking	vs.	Basics
Bob: "We've got to help kids cope with today's complex world, and that means helping them learn how to think out a problem and how to learn what they don't know."		Marian: "The kids can't even remember the basic stuff. They don't even know the dates of the Civil War!"

FIGURE 5.4 *Key Educational Issues*

sidering another person's assumptions about an important issue can broaden one's own thinking and enable one to find common ground with people of different views.

Through discussion of the case and its characters, this section raises participants' awareness of the significance of people's underlying assumptions about key issues.

Ask participants, working in small groups, to select one character and to use the case to develop a character sketch of that person. Encourage participants to think from the character's perspective, and remind them to use the evidence collected in section 1 as a resource. Suggest these questions to focus discussion:

What assumptions about a key issue might this character bring to the task force? (Example: Marian assumes that many students cannot learn beyond the basics and that the need to cover the curriculum leaves no time for higher-order thinking.)

What experiences might have shaped this character's assumptions about a specific issue? (Example: Marian's assumptions about the basics may result from her perceptions of how students have changed, from being isolated in the classroom, from external pressure to finish the text, from concern about students' standardized testing performance.)

Ask each group to share its work. If two groups have selected the same character, compare the similarities and differences in their ideas. After each group has shared its work, ask participants, working in pairs, to select a conversation from the case that relates to an issue or concern in their school. Discuss these questions:

What are your own assumptions about this issue?

How are your assumptions influenced and formed by your educational and personal experiences?

3. Building Consensus. Resolving important issues that evoke strong personal feelings and commitments is a complex process. Through continued discussion of the case and its characters, participants learn about the process of building consensus by articulating points of common understanding and concern and establishing shared values.

Ask participants to work in small groups and to select a key issue that polarizes the characters on the task force.

What are some common concerns that characters have about this issue? (Example: Although Marian and Judith differ on the issue of higher-order thinking versus basics, they are both concerned about how to establish an educational environment that takes students seriously; they are concerned about how to provide maximum support for students.)

Engage participants in a discussion about the meaning and process of consensus. Suggest that they consider how consensus can be built, not by compromising one's beliefs on a given issue but rather by finding common values. Focus discussion with the following questions:

What are the points of agreement between two or more characters? Use the case, information from previous sections, and your own ideas to infer what these characters' shared values might be. (Example: Both Marian and Judith value students' succeeding and have high expectations for them.)

How might these characters use their shared values to work toward consensus on a given issue?

How might this type of consensus building benefit the task force? What next steps do you propose the task force take to come to agreement on certain issues?

How do you view this process of consensus building? What are the key benefits for you, given your own circumstances? What are the possible disadvantages? How might you overcome them? (Example: This process is more about finding common values and less about asking people to compromise on strongly held beliefs. This would work well at a school with a polarized faculty.)

What are some issues in your school that engender polarity? What are some divergent assumptions about these issues? What are some shared concerns and values? How would you go about building consensus around one of these issues?

4. Articulating a Vision. In this section, participants identify a key issue about which they feel most strongly. After considering how they would achieve consensus around this issue, participants envision what a classroom or school, grounded in their perspective on this issue, would look like. In addition, participants may create a profile of a student who is a product of their vision.

Participants may work individually, in pairs, or in small groups. Use these questions to focus discussion:

What key issue do you feel most strongly about?

What common values do various constituencies hold on this issue?

Envision your own classroom or school with a curriculum reflecting your values in place. What would the curriculum be like? What would be happening in classrooms? How would teachers be teaching? What would students be doing? If a colleague were to visit your ideal classroom or school one year from implementation of your ideal curriculum reform, what would be most striking?

Create a profile of a student who is a product of your educational vision. What characteristics and attributes does this student have? What skills, knowledge, and dispositions toward learning does he or she possess? Brainstorm, individually, ideas for a student profile, then share answers with other participants who have values similar to yours. Build consensus around the most salient ideas, and share the group's profile with all participants. Discuss the similarities and differences among the profiles.

5. Taking a Second Look. Part II of the case provides participants with an opportunity to revisit the process of examining assumptions, building consensus, and articulating vision by considering the implications of a final issue: the purposes of schooling and the implications for citizenship preparation. Focus discussion by using the following questions for small or large group consideration:

What new issues emerged from reading Part II?

Select one issue and speculate about one or two characters' assumptions regarding this issue.

Consider how the characters' experiences may have shaped their assumptions about the issue.

What are some shared values around this issue? How can the characters build consensus around this issue?

Consider your beliefs about any new issues that emerged in Part II. How do they alter your vision of a classroom or school? How do they change your student profile?

6

DROPPING A STONE
IN THE WATER

The Northeast and Islands Regional Alliance for Mathematics and Science Education Reform was one of ten regional consortia funded in 1992 by the U.S. Department of Education's Dwight D. Eisenhower program to support improvements in mathematics and science education. Regional Alliance services were provided by partner organizations, including Education Development Center (EDC). EDC designed staff development seminars aimed at improving classroom assessment practices at several pilot sites in the region, working with middle school and high school teachers of mathematics and science.

As part of the program, teachers experimented with alternative forms of assessment in their classrooms, analyzed the resulting student work, and discussed with their colleagues the implications of their efforts for classroom, school, and district assessment practices. The focus on assessment offered a lens on issues of alignment of policies and practices throughout the system, a phenomenon represented in "Dropping a Stone in the Water." The case explores how teachers' efforts to promote change in classroom assessment creates ripples elsewhere in the system, involving players at the school, district, and even state levels.

The case is a fictionalized account of a seminar dedicated to improving classroom assessment practices. The seminar, the dilemmas raised, and the ensuing conversations are composites based on the experience of the Regional Alliance pilot sites. The characters are fictional. This case was originally developed for use in Regional Alliance conferences on assessment and has been adapted slightly here. The funding for the development of this case was provided by the Regional Alliance.

Characters

Allison Thompson, eighth-grade teacher
Don Conway, eighth-grade teacher at Allison's school
Gus Krawski, middle school teacher
Charlie Arnott, middle school teacher at Gus's school
Ann Sweeney, seminar leader and assistant professor of education

Glossary

Alignment. Coherence of different policies and practices within a school, district, or even statewide system of education (e.g., curriculum, assessment)

THE CASE

Deborah Bryant and Barbara Miller

The teachers who had already arrived for the seminar on Tuesday afternoon were helping themselves to coffee and cookies at the rear of the library. The room was noisy with chatter.

Allison Thompson and Don Conway, the young teacher from her school, walked over to one of the small round tables with their coffee. "I tried one of the assessment tasks from the last seminar with my eighth graders," commented Allison. "Here's their work on that statistics problem." Allison rifled through her bag, pulled out a stack of student papers, and spread them on the table.

Shaking his head, Don said, "I can't believe the charts these kids made showing their data on this problem. And the explanations they wrote are great!"

"I was really pleased with what they did," Allison replied. "But, you know, it made me wonder if we give kids enough chances like this to show us what they are able to do."

Gus Krawski swung his leg over the chair next to Allison's and sat down. Hearing the end of her comment, he jumped in, "Speaking of what our kids know and are able to do, did you see the paper today?"

"No, not yet. Why?" Allison looked concerned.

"They released the test scores on the state assessment," Gus replied. "And surprise, surprise, the city's eighth graders are near the bottom of the list. Today's editorial page really lit into the schools."

Allison opened her mouth to reply but was interrupted by a loud voice. "Okay, folks, let's get started!" Ann Sweeney, the facilitator, called from the front of the room. Sixteen teachers slowly moved toward the front of the room and settled in at the small tables.

Charlie Arnott, Gus's school colleague, joined Allison, Don, and Gus at the table. The noise of conversation faded to a low hum. Ann smiled and said, "It looks like we're ready to go. Welcome to our last seminar on assessment reform in mathematics."

Dr. Ann Sweeney, an assistant professor of education at a local university, worked for several area school districts as a consultant for professional development with mathematics and science teachers. She had contracted with this district to offer a series of five seminars on assessment reform for middle school mathematics teachers. There was a lot of interest in the district in assessment; it was the latest "hot topic," just as cooperative learning had been last year.

The seminar series was a far cry from many of the other professional development activities offered by the district. Usually, these were one-shot workshops, conducted by "experts" who came, offered a rather prescriptive program, and left. Ann was helping to facilitate something different, more in-depth; her seminar sessions brought pairs of participating teachers from each school together for discussion and learning.

Ann believed that at this point the seminar series was going pretty well. The teachers were having good conversations during seminars, and they seemed to be engaged. They had tried several alternative assessments in their classrooms, such as open-ended questions and performance tasks, and had brought student work on those problems to the seminars. Those felt like really productive sessions, especially when the teachers were looking at student work together to make the discussions more real.

Recently, discussions in the seminars had started to get more complicated, in the sense that teachers were beginning to raise important and difficult concerns. As they tried some alternative forms of assessment in their classrooms (like open-ended questions), they were beginning to raise questions about needing to change some other things they were doing. The new assessments required that students know, and be able to do, different things from traditional classroom tests. A pressing question, raised by many teachers at the end of the last session was, "Are we really testing what we want students to know?"

Ann had asked the teachers to address this issue by doing an assignment with the partner teacher from their school. They were to look at a recent unit taught in one of their classrooms and make a list of what they wanted students to know and be able to do by the end of the unit. They were then to take the accompanying end-of-the-unit test and compare the two. The idea was to see how closely their tests matched what they wanted students to know and be able to do.

Ann was curious about what they'd bring with them today and where the teachers would go with the discussion, especially as this was the last scheduled seminar.

Ann began by asking for initial reports on what they had found from looking at their tests. Allison whispered to Don, and he raised his hand to volunteer. "Okay, let's start with this table first," Ann said.

He sounded tentative as he reported, "Well, Allison and I looked at the end-of-the-chapter test on factoring that I and several other people in our department gave to our eighth graders a couple of weeks ago. When we compared the test to our list of things we wanted students to know and be able to do, we found out that some important things we wanted kids to be able to do, like problem solving and reasoning, weren't represented on the test. Or, at least not in the right proportions."

"Don, tell us more about the specifics of what you found," suggested Ann.

"Well, on this particular test," said Don, "there were twenty questions and four of them were word problems, which tested problem solving. But a student could get 80 percent of the questions without even trying the word problems. And we all know kids do the worst on those—that's why we always put them at the end of the test. If that was what we really wanted kids to know how to do, that would be the whole test."

"You know, Ann," Allison started, "we expected that part of this exercise was intended for us to see whether our tests were aligned with the outcomes we were looking for. So we sort of expected, and knew anyway, that they wouldn't be totally aligned. I mean, we all know that the tests we give don't capture everything we want kids to know and be able to do. But we were sort of surprised at what we saw when we compared our list of outcomes with what we were testing. There was a *big* mismatch."

"Let's hear from the other people at this table. Gus and Charlie, how about you?" Ann asked.

Gus spoke first. "Well, Charlie and I had a big discussion about whether it was important for students to be able to multiply and divide fractions, which was the unit we looked at. We decided in the end that students needed to know how to do that, but that the computation wasn't the most important thing students needed to know about. What we really cared about was whether students knew when to use those operations to solve problems."

Ann saw lots of heads nodding in agreement with Gus's statement. "But tell me, what was on the test you looked at?" she asked.

"It was pretty traditional," said Charlie. "Mostly computation."

"What's going on there, then?" asked Ann. "It doesn't sound like your tests are a good reflection of those values."

DROPPING A STONE IN THE WATER

The room was silent for a minute. Then Gus blurted out, "Well, you know, Ann, I've been thinking about that. One answer would be to simply change our classroom tests. But I just don't think it's that easy. We test this way for a lot of reasons outside of what we think is best for our kids. I know that doesn't sound right, but it's true."

"Okay, well, let's talk about that, then," said Ann. "What are those other influences, Gus?"

"Well, one thing is the standardized test the state gives," Gus replied. "We get scores for our sixth and eighth graders back every year, and there's always pressure on us to bring up those test scores. Those tests focus on computation, and the only way for our kids' scores to go up is for me to focus directly on computation. There are serious consequences for me, the school, and especially for the kids if our test scores go down any more."

"Well, you know as well as I do, Gus, those test scores just aren't important in terms of what kids really know and can do," Allison said quietly.

"Tell that to the school board. *We* still have to answer for it," Gus replied, gesturing to the other teachers.

"I agree, Gus," said Charlie. "Plus, the curriculum scope and sequence dictate that we need to cover these topics every year. We don't have the freedom to decide to teach something new or not to cover something in the curriculum."

"Tell me more," asked Ann. "How does that affect what you do in your classroom?"

"Well, the district pretty much tells us what has to be covered. It's great to say that we should be teaching more than just computation, that we should be spending a lot of time on problem solving, and all this other new stuff. But the fact of the matter is that we need to be at a certain place in the textbook and in the curriculum by the end of the year, and if we start doing other things, we're never going to make it." Charlie folded his arms across his chest.

"There are other ways to look at it, though," Allison chimed in. "Maybe we need to start making some decisions about what's important for the kids to learn, and then figure out what should be in the curriculum we teach."

"That's easy for *you* to say, Allison," Gus snorted. "*Your* principal lets you teach whatever you want, regardless of the scores or the curriculum."

Allison asked quickly, "What exactly do you mean by that, Gus?"

"Nothing personal, Allison," said Gus. "I just mean, you can't ask teachers to take on all the work of changing what they teach, and buck the system without support. My principal cares about test scores. The district cares about test scores. The state . . . well, you get the point. You've got a lot of energy, Allison, and I know you've done a lot of great things with your kids, but those kinds of activities just aren't sustainable without some big changes in the system. Besides, what happens when kids leave your classroom and go on to ninth grade? Nothing's changing at the high school—and those kids won't even be prepared for that situation. The whole system has got to change. One person can't carry it alone."

Allison looked a little irritated. Don leaned over to her and commented under his breath, "You know, Gus has a point. It is really hard to buck the system."

Allison looked at Don, and whispered, "Believe me, I know how hard it is. But you have to start somewhere."

Ann tried to sum up the conversation: "Gus, it sounds like you're saying these issues of alignment have to be addressed outside of the classroom, that each individual teacher can't solve these issues in isolation. Am I hearing you right?"

"You bet," Gus replied. "So I don't feel like I'm in a position to make big changes. I guess that's up to folks like you, Ann."

Ann laughed. "I don't think so, Gus. I'm always happy to share what I'm hearing from you with the folks I work with in the central office. But remember, I'm really an outsider here. So I think the real question here is, especially given that this is our last planned session, what could a group of teachers, a group like this one, do?"

Study Questions

1. What do you see as the central issue(s) in this case?
2. With which character in the case did you find yourself identifying?
3. In response to Ann's question, what could a group of teachers like this one do?

FACILITATOR'S GUIDE

Deborah Bryant and Barbara Miller

Synopsis of Case

A group of middle school mathematics teachers is participating in an ongoing seminar series on alternative assessment, led by a university consultant, Ann Sweeney. The seminar has encouraged them to experiment with alternative forms of classroom assessment (such as open-ended questions). Over the course of the seminar series, as teachers use some of these new methods, they begin to question whether other aspects of their teaching practice need to change to align with these new assessment practices. Ann gives the teachers an assignment to work with another teacher in their school to examine a curricular unit and a unit test to determine the degree of alignment.

As the case begins, teachers gather for a fifth and last seminar, bringing the results of this assignment with them. The case focuses on the discussion of four of these teachers as they debrief: Allison Thompson, Gus Krawski, Don Conway, and Charlie Arnott. All four teachers agree that there is some misalignment of learning goals and current assessments, but they disagree about how those discrepancies should be resolved. Allison advocates teachers changing their practice despite what the system demands, whereas Gus argues that teachers cannot be expected to make important changes in teaching practice when many elements of the system (such as standardized tests and detailed scope and sequence guidelines) don't support these changes. The case ends with a question from the facilitator, Ann, who asks how the group of teachers can address the alignment issues raised.

Major Issues

The purpose of this case is to raise issues about various forms of alignment (or misalignment). Alignment in this case refers to the coherence of different components of a school system in supporting important learning goals for students. The case is designed to engage readers in thinking about alignment in several different ways, including

- Alignment of curriculum, instruction, and assessment in the classroom teacher's individual practice
- Alignment of assessment systems from classroom to school to district to state and national levels
- Alignment of student experience across grade levels and schools

An important subtext of the case is the use of the staff development seminar as a place where teachers come together to experiment with new practices, examine the work that students do, and discuss what they feel is important in student learning. The professional development setting of the case allows other important themes to emerge: how professional development can support teachers in changing their practice and how groups of teachers in a professional development setting can address important issues such as alignment.

Guiding the Discussion

We describe four activities for structuring discussion of the case. One or more of the suggested activities can be used in a particular discussion. If used as they are currently written and sequenced, we think they provide a nice flow that can deepen participants' understanding of the case and the issues it raises. However, facilitators should tailor the format to meet the needs of the participants: the questions and activities offered here should be seen as suggestions, not as a scripted conversation.

1. Focusing on the Issues, a whole group discussion, helps participants to explore the issues raised in the text and to develop a common understanding of the dilemma presented.
2. Analyzing the Characters, a small group discussion and drawing activity, is designed to support analysis of each character's approach to the dilemma presented in the case.
3. Creating a System Map, a small group activity, helps participants to create a visual mapping of the educational system described in the case and to discuss the attendant issues of alignment. This is followed by large group reporting of the issues raised.
4. Considering Next Steps, a whole group discussion, addresses the final challenge posed in the case.

The study questions at the end of the case preview these activities. They are designed so that participants who consider the study questions ahead of time can engage in a richer conversation.

1. Focusing on the Issues. This case offers many issues to consider, and the discussion in this section encourages participants to describe what they see happening in the case and to focus on the key issues raised by the case.

Unless you have a very large group, you may want to work as an entire group rather than breaking down into smaller groups, so that the entire group has a common understanding of the case before beginning other discussions.

Begin by asking for a participant to give a brief description of what happens in the case. Then ask a second participant to add to that description. These first two steps will allow the whole group to hear a recap of the key events in the case.

Then ask the group, What is this case about? The discussion allows the group to develop a common understanding of the dilemma presented by the case.

Follow up by asking, What are the key educational issues in this case? Make a list on an overhead transparency or on flip chart paper of the issues raised. This will allow the group to explore the issues raised by the case. You can expect to see the following kinds of issues generated:

- Aligning texts, classroom assessment, and external assessment with each other and with broader educational goals
- Relation between classroom tests and standardized tests
- Relation between curriculum and assessment
- Teachers' role in changing the system
- Articulation of what students should know across classrooms and from middle to high school

One potential pitfall is that participants tend to want to jump to solving the problem rather than defining it. It will be tempting for participants to begin discussion immediately about what Ann, Gus, or Allison should do (or should have done). There are several strategies for dealing with this tendency. One option is to simply be explicit that you are asking participants to hold off on problem solving temporarily. If participants offer solutions anyway, a good response might be, "Let's come back to that comment at a later point. Right now I'd like us to stay with defining the problem rather than solving it. That will come later in the discussion."

You may be able to take a problem-solving response and ask the participant to turn it into an issue, by asking a facilitative question such as, "So it sounds like the underlying issue behind that suggestion is . . . ." With this additional focusing, the participant may then be able to work backwards to identify an important issue.

Another alternative is to temporarily indulge the temptation to problem-solve by giving participants a minute or two before the discussion to write, silently and independently, a problem-solving response to a question like, "What could a group of teachers like this one do?" or "How should Ann respond to the concerns being raised by Gus?" Then ask participants to put aside these responses and concentrate on problem definition. Later, when you do address problem solving, participants can write down another problem-solving response and compare it with their earlier response. Often responses change dramatically based on the analysis done by the group, and this can point to the advantage of not immediately jumping to problem solving.

2. Analyzing the Characters. The characters in this case have different experiences regarding the system's alignment as well as different approaches to considering the challenges raised by the misalignment of the system. It is worth exploring on a character-by-character basis the various approaches and assumptions about achieving alignment and change. Begin with Allison and Gus, as the case offers the most evidence of their thinking; if time and interest persist, examine Don, Charlie, and Ann.

If you are working with a large group, now might be a good time to arrange participants in smaller groups, either with each group considering the characters in turn, or with each group choosing to look at one of the characters more closely. The guiding questions for this discussion can be given to small groups on a handout or using an overhead projector or flip chart paper:

What are Gus's (or another character's) concerns?

How are those concerns evidenced in the case?

What are Gus's (or another's) underlying beliefs or assumptions about alignment and how alignment approaches bring about change?

Small groups should discuss these questions and then share their ideas with the entire group. At this point in the discussion, you are moving into a closer analysis of the case. You would like participants to move from broad generalizations to analysis based on the evidence provided. Appropriate probing questions for the facilitator to ask at this point include

What is the evidence you see in the case to support that?

Where does Gus (or another character) demonstrate that?

Give evidence of that assumption (e.g., approach, mindset).

Questions that extend the discussion might include

How does that set of beliefs (approaches, mindsets) serve Gus (or another character)?

How does it limit him or her?

To extend the discussion about approaches to change and alignment for each character, have groups produce a drawing, diagram, or flow chart that shows each character's theory about alignment or change. Using a graphical representation will push participants to think more deeply about the various characters' approaches. One simple drawing participants might do would be to show that Gus perceives change as something that happens to him, and Allison perceives it as something that she makes happen, as shown in Figure 6.1. The

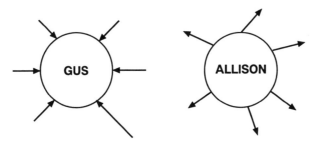

FIGURE 6.1

translation to a visual model may also help support the next activity, if you choose to use it.

3. Creating a System Map. In this activity, participants create a system map to identify various elements of the educational system influencing the classroom; illustrate the relationships among those elements; and analyze connections among various elements in terms of the (mis)alignment of the system. The system map is used as a tool to explore the idea of alignment in the case. An example of a map made during this activity is shown in Figure 6.2.

This kind of activity can easily become very abstract, so to keep it focused (and, in particular, focused on the evidence provided by the case) we suggest that participants be asked to create a map of the influences on one of the characters and the teaching in his or her classroom. The character of Gus provides a rich focus for this activity because the case offers the most information about his situation, and because, as you may already have discussed in the section on character analysis, Gus sees change as happening to him; he is strongly influenced by the characteristics of the system.

This activity works best done in small groups of four or five participants. Use flip chart paper or an overhead transparency for groups to record their mapping, so that the large group can later look at it.

Suggest a center for the map, such as "Gus's classroom." What are the components of the system described in the case that influence the center? Have groups begin to create a map of these ideas or components, using arrows or lines between ideas to indicate relationships. Lead participants through a process for creating a system map, including the following steps:

- Identify the components of the system, as described in the case itself, that influence Gus's classroom (you may want to use Post-it notes or note cards to record these components). What is the evidence in the case about the influences on Gus's classroom?

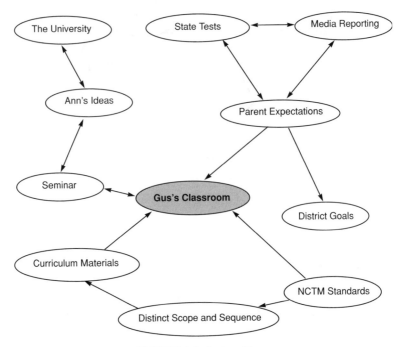

FIGURE 6.2 *System Map*

- Arrange the components in a map to show how they influence Gus's classroom and one another. Participants may suggest that all elements should be connected to all other elements. Encourage them to indicate major or direct relationships.
- Show how elements of the map are connected by using arrows and possibly text to describe the relationships.

The challenge for the facilitator, after the maps have been created, is to prompt discussion of what the maps mean or indicate in terms of alignment. We suggest the following questions to focus this discussion; small groups can address these questions while presenting their maps to the larger group.

What components of the system are in alignment? What are the positive and negative influences on Gus's classroom?

Where does your map indicate that some action needs to be taken to resolve areas of misalignment?

Maps will vary across groups and the variation may provide fodder for further discussion. How are the maps similar? How are they different? What does that say about the issues of alignment? The question about action that needs to be taken provides a natural transition to the next activity, considering next steps for the group of teachers in the case.

4. Considering Next Steps. Once the group has completed a careful analysis of the case, it is appropriate to consider possible answers to Ann's final question. This is a nice opportunity to combine reflective writing with large group discussion. The reflective writing gives participants a chance to reflect individually on their solutions to the dilemma presented by the case. Sharing those thoughts in a large group discussion gives participants a chance to hear, consider, and challenge others' ideas.

Reflective writing and group discussion will go more smoothly with some structure to the activity. We suggest the following sequence.

Give participants five or so minutes to write their responses to the final question Ann raises in the case: What could a group of teachers, a group like this one, do?

Ask participants to share answers with the whole group, recording contributions on flip chart paper or an overhead transparency. To encourage discussion about the solutions offered, use facilitative questions such as

What do others think of that approach?
What would be the benefit of that strategy? the limitations or risks?
Did anyone have a different approach?

To give participants an opportunity to connect the issues in the case to their own situations, you may want to ask them,

In your local context, how could a group of teachers effect change?
How do the issues in the case relate to your own work?

Time permitting, these questions may also be asked:

Is this case realistic?
Have you ever been in a similar situation?

Each individual reacts differently to a case, so be prepared for answers to range from "This would never happen to me" to "I was in a situation exactly like this." Follow up on these comments by probing further and asking participants to describe how such issues play out in their own contexts.

7

WHAT DO WE MEAN BY "SCALING UP"?

The Statewide Systemic Initiative (SSI) program is a major effort by the National Science Foundation (NSF), initiated in 1991, to encourage improvements in science, mathematics, and engineering education through comprehensive systemic change. Under this program, the Maine Mathematics and Science Alliance (MMSA) received a five-year award in 1992. The MMSA proposed to implement improved mathematics and science curricula in seven "Beacon Centers," schools intended to function as laboratories for reform. Each center worked with mathematics and science facilitators to assist with instructional materials, methods, and technology, and it formed a community action team to connect community members to the schools and to the MMSA.

At the time this case was written, in the third year of the grant, the MMSA staff (including the mathematics and science facilitators) faced the challenge of "going to scale"—making the experiences of the Beacon Centers broadly useful to schools throughout the state of Maine and, by extension, throughout the country. "What Do We Mean by 'Scaling Up'?" follows one facilitator as he struggles with this issue. The case explores several possible mindsets about the challenge of "scaling up," making explicit the tension between giving a change effort greater depth and making it broader in reach. Because the issues are complicated, the case is long. The facilitator's guide offers the option of discussing the case in stages.

This case drew upon interviews with those involved in the MMSA, and the characters, events, and conversations are composites. The case was originally written for the SSI community, to encourage conversation around the issue of scale. Funding for the development of the case was provided by the MMSA and the NSF-funded SSI Technical Assistance project at Education Development Center.

Characters

Ben Percy, science facilitator at Maine Beacon Center
Emily Jackson, elementary school teacher
Phyllis Dunlop, middle school principal
Michael Scott, parent with one daughter in a Beacon School
Linda Patterson, marine biologist
Mary Brouillard, math facilitator at Maine Beacon Center
Frank Townsend, staff developer for the Maine Mathematics and Science Alliance

Glossary

Beacon School. Used interchangeably with "Beacon Center"; a school supported by the MMSA and intended to be a laboratory for change in mathematics and science education

Governance team. Each Beacon School is supported by a governance team, which includes members from the school faculty, parents, and the community at large, including higher education and industry

THE CASE

Melinda Fine, Barbara Miller, and Ilene Kantrov

Scene 1—Holiday Inn Meeting Room, Brunswick, Maine

Ben Percy pulled five chairs into a loose circle in the meeting room and eagerly took a seat. He had been looking forward to tonight's meeting of the Beacon Center governance team and felt it was going well so far. He smiled as the team meeting broke into smaller groups so folks could settle in for what he hoped would be some meaty discussions. As one of two staff facilitators for the district's Beacon initiative, Ben felt privileged to have had the opportunity to work with teachers, principals, administrators, and community members for the past three years in supporting their development of more hands-on, problem-solving ways to teach math and science. Ben had been a high school physics teacher in central Maine, and he was known as someone who created challenging activities to pique students' interest—like asking them to design a skull and dropping it from the top of a ladder to see if it would protect a water balloon "brain." The district he now served in this southern coastal region was actually one of seven throughout the state that had been awarded funding through the National Science Foundation (NSF) Statewise Systemic Initiative (SSI) in science, mathematics, and engineering. Tonight's meeting was taking place three years into the project's five-year timeline. The agenda included discussing plans for the fourth year of the project and making decisions to move those plans forward. It seemed an important moment to take stock of where things were and where they should be going.

Emily Jackson, a third-grade teacher from Booker elementary school, took the last seat in the circle and carefully removed the cover from her cup of coffee. "Well, I, for one, feel very good about the work we've done at Booker this past year," she said to the assembled group. "I think we've taken some real steps forward in developing hands-on and problem-solving approaches to math and science"—she paused to take a sip of hot coffee—"and I've been able to collaborate with other teachers in ways I never had before. The projects we've designed have been grounded in real community issues, too, and as a result I think our students have become much more involved and engaged. My feeling is that next year we should basically keep on doing what we've been doing, but just do more of it—that is, bring more and more teachers on board."

Ben leaned forward in his chair and said, "I agree that some very important gains have been made, Emily, and it's been very exciting for me to be a part of them. But it seems to me that the challenge of next year is to go beyond simply bringing more of our own teachers on board. Given where we are in the project, I think we also need to be thinking about scaling up *beyond* our own district. My question is, How do we scale up and still continue the good work we've done up till now?"

"Don't you think it depends on how you define *scaling up*, Ben?" asked Phyllis Dunlop, the principal of Essex Middle School. "Looking around this room, I see evidence of some pretty good scaling up that we've done already."

Ben and the others surveyed the room quickly. Governance team members sat clustered in small groups around the room, already deep in conversation. The governance team was certainly diverse, composed of business people, professors from the nearby university, a college president, local scientists and engineers, parents, a number of teachers, and two school administrators.

"We've reached out to people who've traditionally not been a part of school reform efforts," Phyllis continued, "and who haven't really been encouraged to see what goes on inside schools as their concern. I, for one, have always been frustrated by what I've seen as a huge and unnecessary gap between our schools and the communities they serve. We haven't been very good in the past at really involving outside people in the work we're doing. As a principal, I'd guess my main interaction with parents has been when their kid was in trouble. But that's a waste of great potential. We need to bring parents and others on board up front, and in more substantive ways."

"I'm with you on that," interjected Michael Scott, the father of a ninth-grade girl, "and I think we parents need to learn how to become more involved in those ways, too. We certainly want to support our kids' learning, but we usually haven't had entry points beyond periodic parent conferences and that sort of thing."

"Well, for that matter, we teachers often haven't known how to deepen and sustain parents' interest," Emily Jackson added.

"That's my point exactly!" continued Phyllis. "With the Beacon Center initiative I feel we've really begun to make headway in tackling that gap between the community and the school. Remember our original proposal to become a Beacon site? We had people from all over the community working together to develop that proposal."

"It was really something!" Linda Patterson cut in. She was a marine biologist who'd been collaborating with the Moffet elementary school for over two years. "I worked on it, too, along with a few of my colleagues from the lab. About one hundred folks overall were involved, from discussion groups to actually writing the proposal. And many of us are still very active."

"Uh huh," continued Phyllis, "and the technology grant is another case in point. You were involved with that, weren't you, Emily?" Emily nodded. "Well, correct me if I'm wrong, but as I understand it, that whole project came out of our need to develop better communication among folks throughout the district, and to develop ways to really deepen community involvement."

"That's right," Emily replied. "And the team that pulled together that grant included several other teachers, too, along with parents, people working in technology, some local business leaders, the director of the library main branch—just loads of folks. That collaboration was really powerful. I think it's why we were awarded a million dollars to help us develop an electronic network for the district."

"So now we have the capacity to develop all sorts of wonderful things," Phyllis continued, "like computer hookups so parents can have direct access to teachers in their kids' schools; community bulletin boards to keep all of us better informed about what's going on; expanded access to the library; electronic avenues for students to pose questions directly to math and science experts and to local business people, too; an expanded resource base for teachers—you name it. Everyone is excited about learning to use this technology. But I think the excitement's also about our coming together on behalf of our kids." She turned in her chair to face Ben directly. "If scaling up is about reaching out to more people so reform efforts can deepen and grow, we've certainly been doing that here."

Ben shifted uncomfortably in his seat. He agreed with Phyllis that the initiatives she mentioned were important—if unusual—ways to think about scaling up. But he believed scaling up meant something else as well, something closer to what the NSF and the Maine Department of Education had in mind when they talked about spreading reform beyond the seven districts served most directly by the Beacon Centers. He responded somewhat tentatively. "What you say is really important, Phyllis, and those accomplishments shouldn't be overlooked. I guess what I'm trying to push us on is how we can share what we've learned with others in the state, and how we can also learn more from the experience of other districts."

"Look, I'm all for 'sharing,'" Michael responded testily, "but the sharing I want to do is with folks here at home." He glanced around the group, looking for signs of support. "I didn't really know anything about these new teaching approaches until last fall, when my daughter, Elizabeth, started coming home from school all excited about a recycling project her class was involved in. My wife and I were so pleased. Lizzie's a good student, but she's never been motivated by math and science before. So I asked her what all the fuss was about—why she was so gung ho all of a sudden—and she told me that *this* year the work really mattered, that her project could actually help the town. The practical nature of the work meant a real lot to her."

"That's wonderful, Michael," Linda volunteered supportively. "I've heard other parents say that sort of thing about the work I've done with their kids at the Moffet School, too, and it's been very gratifying. But what's wrong with sharing that sort of thing beyond our district? You seem to be suggesting that there's some sort of conflict there."

"Well, I just don't think we have the time to reach out to everyone!" Michael answered with passion. "Look, we've been a Beacon site for three years, and my daughter didn't get a teacher who's really taking this stuff to heart until this year. That's two years of missed opportunities for her. I just think we should be reaching all of our own kids through all of our own teachers before we start looking farther afield."

"The problem is that the district is too big to reach everybody at once," Emily explained. "We work in teams in the schools, and we rotate in new teachers every academic year so we can eventually reach the entire teaching staff. But we've had to do it gradually."

"I understand that," Michael continued. "But my point is that we should continue to focus in our own backyards, where our own tax dollars are going to be spent, before we go over into somebody else's." Linda nodded her head thoughtfully. "And it's not just more teachers and more kids that we need to bring on board," Michael continued. "It's more parents, too. Before, my daughter started getting the Beacon newsletter, but in all honesty I didn't pay much attention. Then Lizzie started getting excited, and she took us to a 'Family Math and Science' night last fall. Now look at me! I'm one of two parents running the program!"

"And you're stuck here on a Thursday night," Linda continued humorously, "missing your favorite TV show to debate fourth-year plans with your esteemed colleagues on the Beacon Center governance team!"

Everyone laughed. Linda's comment seemed to diffuse an undercurrent of tension in the group, and Ben took advantage of the opening. He asked Michael sincerely, "What's worked for you with 'Family Math and Science?' Why do you think it's been so powerful?"

"Well, I've really enjoyed joining my daughter in doing math and science exercises, and in learning alongside of her. Last month we had close to 70 parents and their kids using mini-marshmallows to calculate the volume of different containers. The energy in the room was infectious."

"Holding these nights in McDonald's is a great idea," Phyllis contributed. "The atmosphere is so friendly. It seems to really help bridge that school/community split."

"Yeah," continued Michael, "and I think our kids get a kick out of our joining them. You know it's probably good for them to see that their old Mom and Dad can still learn a thing or two, right along with them!"

"It's great that you've taken so much initiative with the program," Emily Jackson noted appreciatively. "The parents I know who've done it share your enthusiasm." She paused, furrowing her brow. "I actually wanted us to get back to what Ben was saying earlier—that it's not just a question of what we have to share with other districts, but of what we have to learn from them, too. Because I see a number of different sides to this issue, and I'm trying to sort them through. You see," Emily continued, looking at Michael, "I just did a presentation on some of the work we've been doing at a conference in Augusta. There were about 350 teachers there from all across the state who came together to share models of good teaching practice. It was a fantastic experience for me. I learned a tremendous amount about different ways to do things, and about math and science as well. And I came back fired up with new ideas to share with my students. I guess you'd say that that conference was my first official 'scaling up' experience, since I went there to disseminate information about our work to non-Beacon teachers and administrators. But I came back feeling that I got at least as much as I gave. It wasn't an information dump, you see, it was a real back and forth where each side felt enriched by having worked with the other."

"I'm glad you feel that way about it, Emily," Ben commented. "I remember asking you to present something at last year's conference, and you fought me tooth and nail."

"You're absolutely right!" Emily responded, laughing. "Because things just felt too new for me back then. But you hung in with me, and with your support, and with the support of other teachers I've been teaming with, I got to a place this year where I felt like I really had something to share."

Ben smiled warmly, appreciative of Emily's growth and touched that she had acknowledged his role in it.

"But it's taken me a really long time to get to this place, Ben," Emily continued, "and that's why I see Michael's point, too. We seem to have this frustrating trade-off. We work in focused ways with small groups of teachers, and those of us who are lucky enough to be involved gradually learn to change. But we still haven't reached lots of our staff, much less all the teachers in the district. So that means there are very different types of practice going on at the same time, and the reforms feel more like pockets of activity than like anything systemic. Frankly, my biggest fear is that we won't have brought enough of our own teachers on board to make a permanent change in school culture—one that we can sustain beyond the five years of NSF funding."

Ben looked puzzled. "I'm not sure I follow you, Emily. Do you think we should be less focused on concentrated work with teams of teachers at this point, and more expansive in our reach? Is it that the rotation system isn't working to bring more people in, or . . . ?"

"It's working, it's working," Phyllis interrupted a bit impatiently. "But I think what Emily is saying is that the need is so urgent that it just feels like we can never do it fast enough. You know, at the latest state professional meeting of principals I attended, many of us talked a lot about what's been happening in our Beacon schools. We're proud of what's going on, and we want to share our successes with our colleagues across the state. We're even willing to discuss our problems, and to talk about how far we still have to go. But it's a question of limited resources, of where we should be putting most of our efforts." She turned toward Emily and said, "I really share your concern about whether we'll be able to sustain the effort beyond the funding period." Phyllis looked at Ben. "And in all honesty, I'm nervous about the fact that you'll be devoting less of your time to our district over the next two years. I want more of your time, Ben, not less. More on-site training for our entire staff, and less of these short-term projects with small groups of teachers. You see, we need a critical mass of teachers to make a long-term impact. I know we need that in our school, and I think we need it in all the schools across the district."

Linda jumped in. "But the reality is, we're going to get less of Ben's time, not more, over the next two years. Look, folks, we all knew this was coming. We even planned for it in our proposal. We told the NSF that by the fourth year we'd be lessening our reliance on our two staff facilitators, planning for how we'd be sustaining our efforts once the funding runs out."

"That's part of what's behind my bringing the issue up tonight," Ben acknowledged. "The NSF wants to see evidence of 'systemic-ness,' evidence that the initiatives we've been implementing are beginning to reach a broader body of people."

"I appreciate the pressure you're all under, Ben," Linda continued, "but with all due respect, the impetus for scaling up has to be internal or we're not going to get anywhere. I realize the NSF funds projects all across the country, but in this state the game is local control. We control our kids' educational agenda, not the federal government or even the state. So we on the local level have to see reaching out as something that's in our best interest, or we're simply not going to do it."

"Well, I don't see how we can possibly see it that way," Michael commented. "It's not that I'm against scaling up in a philosophical sense. But from a practical standpoint, how can it possibly benefit us to divert our energies from our own backyard?"

"Well, practically speaking," Linda responded, "it's a question of resources, as Phyllis says. But maybe it's also a question of the *type* of resources we're talking about. If we think of scaling up as an information exchange rather than an information dump—as Emily experienced it at that conference she went to—then we open ourselves up to a greater pool of resources by working with folks beyond our own district. Come to think of it, maybe it's not all that different from what we've gained by narrowing the gap between the school and the community."

"I'm not sure I follow you," rejoined Phyllis. "Can you say more?"

"Well, you've already spoken about the power that's come from involving community members in more substantive ways. In the past, parents and other community people would typically have been brought in for a 'show-and-tell' deal, something like, 'Hi kids, I'm Linda Patterson, a marine biologist. My work consists of blah blah blah.' That sort of thing. Look, I did those kinds of presentations before, and they were fine, but they didn't make me feel that the 'concerns of the school were my own,' as you yourself said. Well, now for the past two years I've been acting as a 'community colleague' with the Moffet School, and I've been sitting down with teachers and helping to plan curricular units. It's been wonderful, because together we've developed year-long themes around studying the marine life of Maine. Students have learned about aquaculture through raising their own seed clams. They've visited the Maine coastline and made observations of various species. We even received a one-thousand-dollar grant to purchase a saltwater aquarium for the school, and now the kids are developing feeding studies of the organisms in the aquarium. All I'm suggesting, Phyllis, is that engaging folks in regions *beyond* our own district might be one way to maximize the power of the *people* resources that are out there. And that, in turn, Michael, might help us strengthen the work we're doing within our own backyards." Linda relaxed back in her chair and shrugged her shoulders. "Look, Maine is a poor state. Our material resources have always been limited. So let's use our good old Yankee ingenuity here. There's got to be some way to bridge our immediate and longer-term needs." She concluded by posing a question directly to Ben. "Do you have any ideas for how we can bridge these things, Ben?" she asked. "Where do you stand on all of this?"

"In all honesty, I'm not sure I know at this point," answered Ben. "I agree with most of what has been said tonight, and I'm struggling with how to put it all together to help move us forward."

Scene 2—Joey's Diner, Topsham, Maine

Ben took a bite of his glazed doughnut and began flipping through the notes he'd taken during last night's meeting. He'd had a somewhat restless night, unable to get his mind off the discussion. He was feeling a bit confused about his own response. Why was he feeling so frustrated by people's hesitation to reach beyond their district? For that matter, why was he feeling troubled by people's expressed reliance on *him*?

Ben wondered how the small group discussion had gone for Mary Brouillard, the math facilitator with whom he worked at the Beacon site, and for Frank Townsend, the staff person he worked with most closely at the Augusta office that managed the SSI statewide. He looked out the window of the diner, searching for Mary's and Frank's cars in the parking lot. Not here yet. He took a sip of hot coffee and returned to his notes.

Ben had been pleased to learn that Emily was feeling so good about the work they'd been doing together for the past three years. He, too, had felt that impressive gains had been made in what he now saw as a relatively brief period of time. He mentally ticked off evidence of progress. Projects grew out of real community issues—the need for recycling local waste; the importance of protecting the soil and water quality of Maine's largest saltwater bay; determining appropriate methods for measuring potato quality during the annual potato harvest. Community leaders from all walks of life had begun to work directly with schools, giving folks a real stake in their public schools and helping to ensure that students' learning was grounded and useful. Teachers were working together to develop, plan, and implement innovative programs. And perhaps most important, students seemed genuinely excited by these new approaches, and girls as well as boys were taking initiative in designing and carrying out problem-solving and hands-on math and science projects.

Why was it going so well? Ben read through Phyllis's comments of the night before, trying his best to decipher his own hurried scrawl. He agreed that they'd been successful in reaching out to people whom they'd never reached before, and that they had, in fact, involved these folks in new and important ways. And Phyllis was quite right to identify their approach as a form of scaling up. Ben himself had always been bothered by the "depth versus breadth" argument that people wrangled over in meetings—the notion that one can't reach "in" to the community and "out" beyond the community simultaneously. Phyllis seemed to offer an escape from this quagmire by identifying how they'd reached out to new people throughout the district even as they'd deepened the opportunities these people had for a genuinely meaningful involvement.

Why couldn't reaching *beyond* the district be viewed in this same light? Michael had made no bones about the fact that he saw local work as conflicting with efforts directed beyond the district. At points Emily seemed to second Michael's point of view, even though she had understood from her own conference experience that scaling up could be a two-way street. Linda was right on target, he thought, when she said that the impetus for scaling up had to be internal or it would never get anywhere. So what would it take to get folks to generalize from Emily's experience—to see that scaling up beyond the district had value for their own work back home?

Ben looked at his watch and wondered what was keeping Mary and Frank. He was feeling uncharacteristically impatient, and he wondered again why last night's meeting bothered him as much as it did. He found Michael's and Phyllis's comments the most difficult to take in. Michael's argument against folks diverting their energies from their own backyard seemed to imply that it was someone else's responsibility to scale up beyond one's district, not that of the teachers or principals or parents or community members within the Beacon sites. Whose responsibility then—his?

At the same time, Phyllis had made him feel that he was somehow abandoning ship to work increasingly with non-Beacon districts in the remaining two years of the project. Perhaps she would feel less reliant on him if she could see Linda's position—that bringing folks in from beyond the district could bring new people resources into the community.

But was his own presence really so crucial? Other people seemed equally essential—Linda with all the work she was doing with the Moffet School; Michael with his actually running the "Family Math and Science" program; Emily with her tireless commitment to train more and more teachers across the district; and so many more. These people would surely continue with their work whether he was there or not. Were the changes less systemic than he had thought, then? Or had he not done enough to build people's own capacity to rely on themselves? Ben stared out the window, deep in thought.

Scene 3—Joey's Diner, Topsham, Maine

Mary and Frank arrived at the parking lot simultaneously and headed into the diner, unnoticed by Ben. "Hello there, pal," Mary said warmly as she slid into the booth beside him. Mary and Ben had worked together closely for nearly three years now. She knew him to be a thoughtful man who took his work very seriously. "You look far away. How did it go last night with your group?"

"I'm not entirely sure," Ben answered with a slight chuckle. "I was counting on you guys to help me figure that out." Mary smiled. Frank took a seat, reached into his briefcase to pull out his own notes from last night, and replied, "I'm game."

"Well, without going over the entire discussion," Ben said, "I guess it'd be fair to say that it more or less boiled down to conflicting views about scaling up that people within our group put forward. Some felt that we've been successful in scaling up so far because we've involved lots of community players in our initiative. Others felt there was real value to be gained by our reaching out more to folks *beyond* the district. And another person—a parent—felt that any effort to reach beyond the district would drain our energy and resources."

"Sounds complicated," Mary said.

"It was. And what troubles me is the fact that I personally don't see a conflict between how we've involved lots of community players up till now and how we might approach reaching out beyond the district next year," Ben answered. "And the fact that a few folks were afraid that if your focus and mine shifted, Mary, then the progress within the district might not be sustained. And also the fact that some seemed to see 'reaching out' as our responsibility rather than theirs."

"The responsibility issue *is* key," Mary agreed, sounding troubled. "You know, Ben, I think we've really succeeded in helping teachers and others in the community look at math and science in new ways, but it seems to me that our greatest challenge this year will be to make ourselves more dispensable."

"I agree," Ben said, "but how?"

"By helping people feel more ownership of the Beacon project overall," Mary continued, "and by helping them see how much they have to share with each other. By empowering them so they'll see that they can answer questions without relying on us. *That's* how this work will be sustained beyond year five."

"But teachers and other community players have to see there's value in that ownership for themselves," Ben added, "or the views of folks like the father who spoke in my group will hold sway."

"I suspect they won't see that value until they get something back from what they're giving," Frank contributed." And some of the so-called scaling up initiatives we've got going may do just that. Take the technology grant you all shepherded through, for example. Once the Internet and World Wide Web link is up and running, teacher-to-teacher communication will be possible in a way it hasn't been before, and through a network that's ongoing, too. Teachers will be able to share what they know, and to ask questions of people all over the country. That will lessen their reliance on you both and help spread some good ideas besides."

"There's another example that came up in my group last night, too," Mary contributed. "We had an eighth-grade math teacher who'd participated in an academy last summer, and she spoke very enthusiastically about her experience."

"Which academy had she done?" asked Frank.

"That three-week one with the 'Watersheds' theme that we ran out of Baldwin Community College," answered Mary. "This teacher said she'd been—now what was her word?—'re-energized' by working with Baldwin faculty last summer, because her own content knowledge had been terrifically enriched. She also felt she'd benefited by having had the opportunity to stay in contact with other academy participants throughout the year."

"Opportunity is a nice way to see it," noted Ben, "since we *require* them to stay in contact."

"Well, apparently she tried out a number of the experiential learning activities she'd done last summer with her own students this year," said Mary. "And she felt it had been very useful to meet periodically with her academy colleagues to discuss what worked and what didn't, to trouble-shoot, and to learn what the other teachers had and hadn't done."

"You see," Ben interjected, "that's exactly why I don't see our reaching out *beyond* Beacon districts as being all that different from how we reach more deeply *within* them. These academies are definitely an attempt to scale up sound practice, and like the Beacon work, they build in collaboration with some unusual players—in this instance, institutions of higher learning. They also promote meaningful, ongoing collaborations across Beacon and non-Beacon sites. How do you see them fitting in, Frank, from the statewide perspective?"

"Well, the academies do seem to meld the NSF's concern for reaching out to more people with the Beacon's emphasis on bringing in different stakeholders, promoting ongoing collaboration, and allowing for local adaptation. We've typically pulled in about 85 percent of our participants from non-Beacon districts. As a result, in the first two years of the project, I'd say that we've affected at least twelve thousand kids—maybe as many as fifteen thousand kids—from close to one hundred towns throughout Maine."

"Maybe the success of the academies points to our need to shift how we pitch what scaling up is about," Ben conjectured. "It's not dissemination, it's collaboration. And it's also about creating opportunities for people to say, 'This is what we've learned, and what's useful in it. It may not fit your situation exactly, but here are some good components of it.'"

"You can't short-circuit the process," cautioned Mary. "Each community has to go through its own process to be able to change."

"Of course," Ben added, "and each needs to work with more than the usual suspects to make that happen."

"We're constructing a very big conception of scaling up here," observed Frank. "It may give us a more useful way to think about how responsibility can be shared and where value can be found."

"But it still feels like we're assembling the plane while we're flying it," Ben acknowledged. "So where do we go in terms of our planning for the next few years?"

FACILITATOR'S GUIDE

Deborah Bryant and Barbara Miller

Synopsis of Case

For the past three years, Ben Percy, a staff facilitator in Maine, has been working with teachers, administrators, and community people in advancing more hands-on, problem-solving ways to teach math and science in grades K–16. Ben's efforts support one of Maine's seven Beacon Centers—sites of innovative practice funded by the National Science Foundation (NSF) Statewide Systemic Initiative (SSI). Three years into the project's five-year timeline, members of one Beacon Center governance team meet to take stock of progress made thus far and to address priorities for years four and five of the project.

The discussion quickly turns to the issue of "scaling up" innovative practice. Numerous, and at times conflicting, conceptions of scaling up are put forward by various members of the group. Some define *scaling up* as reaching deeply *within* the district to involve diverse stakeholders in the initiative; others define it as reaching *beyond* the district to collaborate with or bring new players on board. Some see reaching "in" as a priority and reaching "out" as a drain on energy and resources; others believe energy and resources will be expanded by collaborating with people beyond the Beacon site. Several are concerned that reform must become more systemic in order to be sustained beyond the NSF funding period.

Troubled by the discussion, Ben turns to two of his colleagues who attended the meeting but participated in other small groups' discussions. The three point to additional examples of how scaling up has occurred throughout the state and discuss what it might take to help governance team members see reaching "in" and "out" as complementary, rather than competing, activities. They also discuss how to foster a greater sense of responsibility for scaling up among the individuals directly involved in reform—teachers, administrators, and community members. In keeping with some in Ben's group, they propose a scaling up model that emphasizes collaboration rather than dissemination, but they are still left wondering how to proceed in the remaining two years of the project.

Major Issues

The purpose of this case is to promote discussion about issues that arise when people deeply involved in reform efforts think about what it means to scale up innovative practice. The case is designed to engage participants in thinking about various dimensions of scaling up, including

- Different understandings of what it means to scale up (e.g., reaching "in" and reaching "out")
- Different models for scaling up (e.g., a collaboration approach versus a dissemination approach)
- Building a sense of shared responsibility for scaling-up efforts
- Increasing local ownership of the change process
- Bringing added value to communities involved in the scaling-up change process
- Capacity building to sustain systemic change

Guiding the Discussion

Discussion of this case and of the issues it raises can proceed in different ways, depending on the needs and experiences of the participants. The activities and questions offered here provide several ways to structure a conversation around scaling up and larger systemic reform issues. One possibility is to follow the six activities as described here; they are sequenced to build the discussion from close attention to the story line to broader consideration of the issues raised in the case. However, do not feel limited to the activities or chronology described here, and do not feel compelled to include all the activities. Decide which activities to use, and in which order, based on your purpose for the discussion and the needs and interests of your audience.

1. Focusing on the Issues, a whole group discussion, helps participants to focus on the main issues in the case and to develop a common understanding of its central dilemma.
2. Understanding Perspectives, a small group discussion, supports participants in developing an understanding of the variety of perspectives on scaling up contained in the case.
3. Creating Images, a small group activity, leads participants to create visual images for scaling up and then to share those images in the larger group.
4. Looking at the Bigger Picture is a large or small group discussion of the larger systemic reform issues in the case.
5. Exploring Facilitation is a small or large group discussion of the role of the facilitator, Ben, in the central dilemma of the case.
6. Considering Next Steps is a large group discussion of the possible next steps the characters in the case could take to resolve the central dilemma.

As you will notice, this case is longer than other cases you may have used. This is both an opportunity and a challenge for facilitators. The length and depth of the case provide a rich field for discussion and, at the same time, the potential for far-ranging discussion to address the many issues and perspectives contained in the case. The challenge is to remain focused and to keep track of the different threads in the discussion.

In most instances, it will be advantageous to discuss the case in parts, to make the discussion more manageable. The discussion guide breaks the case down into two parts, the first part containing scenes 1 and 2, and the second part scene 3.

Have participants read scenes 1 and 2 before beginning the case discussion, and use the activities Focusing on the Issues, Understanding Perspectives, Creating Images, and Looking at the Bigger Picture. Then have participants read scene 3, and use the activities Exploring Facilitation and Considering Next Steps.

We recommend this approach because scene 3 marks a shift to issues faced by systemic reform facilitators, particularly in highlighting some of the internal dilemmas and speculations of the main character, Ben. Considering Next Steps will of course prompt more fruitful discussion when participants have read the entire case.

1. Focusing on the Issues. It is often helpful to begin a case discussion with an opportunity for the whole group to develop a common understanding of the breadth of issues in the case. Discussion in this section encourages participants to articulate problems and issues in the case, and to develop some common expectations around various terms used in the case. Because the intent is to create some common understandings, it can be helpful to engage the whole group in this part, even if you intend to spend most of the discussion time working in smaller groups.

Providing a focus on the key issues in the case is particularly important with a case as context-rich, detailed, and lengthy as this one. Use the following questions to guide this part of the discussion:

- What is the central problem in this case? Allow a variety of responses, to generate multiple ideas of the key problem in the case. The case is rich enough to allow several possible descriptions of the key dilemma. Follow up with questions such as, Whose problem is it?
- What are the buzzwords or phrases characters use to talk about scaling up? This question begins to focus on the various perspectives on scaling up contained in the case.
- What comments or ideas raised in the case did you find most compelling? Follow up with questions such as, Why? Can you give an example from the text where you see evidence of that?

It is helpful for the facilitator or an assistant to record responses on an overhead transparency or flip chart paper. This creates a visual record of the conversation and contributes to the development of a common understanding of the dilemmas in the case. Often, recording comments in this manner can create an opportunity for the facilitator to reflect back meaning to the speaker or ask for clarification.

WHAT DO WE MEAN BY "SCALING UP"?

A natural pitfall for participants at this point in the discussion is to want to offer solutions for the main character, in this case Ben. The challenge for the facilitator is to keep participants on track in defining the problem and resisting the temptation to problem-solve too quickly.

2. Understanding Perspectives. Focusing on a particular character offers participants the opportunity to look closely at various scaling-up issues and to consider the ways in which those issues are understood by other characters in the case. In this activity, participants work in small and large groups to articulate and analyze the perspectives of the characters regarding scaling up.

Small group discussion. This is an ideal time for participants to work in small groups, for an in-depth discussion. Each small group should choose one character to analyze. This case offers many possible characters to analyze. Michael Scott, Linda Patterson, and Emily Jackson are good choices because they offer sufficient evidence in the case of their approaches to scaling up and because they represent a range of roles. It may be useful to refrain from an analysis of Ben Percy's perspective until the activity Exploring Facilitation. If you are not using that activity, then it would make sense to include Ben as a character for the present activity.

Do not feel compelled to analyze every character in the case. It is more useful to get an in-depth look at some perspectives rather than a complete analysis of all the characters. If you have six small groups focusing on these characters, you might ask pairs of groups to look at the same character, rather than asking each group to analyze a different character. The narrower focus (on three rather than six characters) will make the small group reporting more manageable.

The guiding questions for the discussion should be introduced by the facilitator and then left on the overhead projector or flip chart paper for groups to refer back to.

What is Linda's (or Emily's or Michael's . . .) view of scaling up? What does scaling up mean for him/her? What evidence from the text illustrates this perspective?

How might Linda's (or Emily's or Michael's . . .) perspective on scaling up be shaped by her/his role (teacher, administrator, parent/volunteer, community member)?

How has Linda's (or Emily's or Michael's . . .) perspective changed during the time s/he has worked with the Beacon Center? In what ways?

What problem or issue is most troubling to Linda (or Emily or Michael . . .)? Why?

Large group discussion. Provide an opportunity for the small groups to report to the large group about each character. In order to keep the analysis of characters close to the text, consider these follow-up questions:

What evidence do you see in the case to support that?

Where does the character demonstrate that?

This discussion can be extended beyond the evidence of the text to include consideration of how a particular perspective forms a character's perceptions and experiences. Push participants to extend their descriptions of the characters with questions such as

How does that perspective serve this character? How does it shape his/her perception of the problem in the case?

How does it limit this character? What is s/he not focused on or aware of in this case?

In the large group (or by bringing two or three small groups together), focus on the similarities and differences among characters' perspectives on scaling up.

Which characters share similar views? In what ways?

In what ways are characters' roles linked to different perspectives on scaling up?

Identifying with characters. As a facilitator, one issue to consider is the extent to which participants are able to connect personally to the case. Do they see themselves in the role of one of the characters in the case? If you feel that some participants may be having trouble making that connection, a few facilitative questions may help bridge the gap.

For instance, suppose you are using this case with an audience that includes university preservice educators, and you are aware that they might not feel as connected to the case as some other participants, since none of the characters in the case are described as preservice educators. You may then want to focus in particular on the facilitative question of how characters' roles are linked to their perspectives. You may want to ask specifically how the perspective of a preservice educator adds a new dimension to the case, and encourage some discussion of that question.

Personal identification with the case can be extended through reflective writing. Ask participants to write for five minutes individually on the following questions:

With which character's perspective do you most identify?

How is your perspective similar to and different from that character's?

If time allows, ask participants to share some of their responses.

3. Creating Images. *Scaling-up* is a term that lends itself to visual interpretation. In this section, participants are asked to sketch various images of scaling up. This activity can open up new ideas about the issue, point out pitfalls in traditional conceptions of scaling up, and illustrate different and sometimes competing values about scaling up.

Provide colored markers, crayons, or transparency pens, and ask participants to sketch on pieces of newsprint or overhead transparencies in response to the following questions:

What do you believe is a traditional image of scaling up?

What is a different way to portray some aspect of scaling up that is reflected in this case?

You might ask each individual in the large group to sketch and share traditional images of scaling up. Then, as individuals or in small groups, have participants produce drawings of alternative images of scaling up present in the case. Encourage participants to think of themselves as creating preparatory sketches, as an artist would do, rather than creating a finished product. One facilitator who used this activity successfully allowed participants five minutes to work individually to generate some ideas, then had them share those ideas in pairs, and then in groups of six to create a group image.

After everyone has finished sketching, look as a large group at the images created. Use the following questions to extend the conversation:

Are the traditional images of scaling up similar or different in important ways?

What are the challenges of traditional images of scaling up?

What new aspects of scaling up are conveyed by the other sketches people created?

How are the various images of scaling up similar and different?

In what ways might various sketches be combined?

4. Looking at the Bigger Picture. Moving beyond the issues mentioned explicitly in the case, this section frames questions about a larger set of systemic reform issues. It provides an opportunity to set the case in the context in which you are working. How do the issues of scaling up and the accompanying systemic challenges apply to the reform context in your school, district, or larger system?

Focus the discussion on the idea of scaling up a particular innovation that is being supported in your context. The questions presented here are framed in a general fashion. You are encouraged to adapt them to fit the particular reform context in which you and the participants are working.

Working in a small or large group format, participants may consider the following questions:

What is the innovation?

What is the "added value" of the innovation that would make it a candidate for scaling up?

Why is it challenging to maintain the intellectual integrity of an innovation or idea when it moves beyond the place where it originated? What strategies can be used to maintain that integrity?

To extend the discussion, participants might consider their expectations for various individuals involved in scaling up. For instance, those who originate an idea often have a deeper experience and are more likely to maintain the innovation, compared with those who "receive" an innovation. Additional questions include

When scaling up an innovation you initiated, what kind of experience do you hope others will have?

What does it mean to originate rather than "receive" an innovation? What are the differences between collaboration and dissemination as models for scaling up?

5. Exploring Facilitation. For use after reading scene 3, this section focuses on the nature of facilitation to support scaling-up efforts. This is an opportunity to analyze and understand the perspective of Ben, the facilitator featured in the case. He is pulled in two directions: one, still trying to carry on his current work, and two, looking to reach out beyond the community. He feels that the demand for his support is greater than he can respond to, so he is trying to build the capacity of others.

At the beginning of the discussion of scene 3, return to defining the problem, this time from Ben's perspective. Ask the large group to answer the following questions, again recording comments on flip chart paper or an overhead transparency:

After the governance team meeting, upon reflection, what does Ben see as the problem?
How does he articulate it to Frank and Mary?
How is Ben feeling about this dilemma?

This will help the group develop a common understanding about the dilemmas Ben faces. Now ask participants to discuss the following questions in smaller groups:

What were Ben's assumptions about his role as a facilitator during the first few years?
What are his assumptions about his role at the time of the case?
What constitutes success for Ben as a facilitator at this point in his work?
What support does Ben need to continue his work as a facilitator committed to scaling up?

In the large group, share responses to these questions. Extend the conversation about support for Ben with questions such as the following:

If you were Mary, Frank, or other staff Ben works with, how would you support Ben?
How could people in other sectors (e.g., higher education, community) support Ben?
If you were Ben, what sort of support should you seek out?

6. Considering Next Steps. Once the group has completed a careful analysis of the case, as described in the preceding activities, it is appropriate to consider some solutions to the dilemmas described.

Moving beyond the story line of the case, this section asks participants to offer ideas about possible next steps. Have participants first work individually, writing responses to the following questions. Then move to small or large group discussion. Sharing these thoughts in a discussion gives participants a chance to hear, consider, challenge, and extend others' ideas.

What might Ben, Mary, and Frank take as a next step with the governance teams?

What are some elements of a plan for scaling up with which most, if not all, of the governance team would agree?

Encourage discussion of the solutions offered by asking facilitative questions such as the following:

What would be the benefits of that strategy? What would be the limitations or risks?

What issues related to scaling up seem most important to address in the next steps?

BIBLIOGRAPHY

Barnett, C., D. Goldenstein, and B. Jackson. 1994. *Fractions, Decimals, Ratios, and Percents: Hard to Teach and Hard to Learn*, Facilitator's Discussion Guide. Portsmouth, NH: Heinemann.

Barnett, C., and S. Sather. 1992. "Using Case Discussions to Promote Changes in Beliefs among Mathematics Teachers." Unpublished manuscript presented at American Educational Research Association Annual Meeting, San Francisco.

Cohen, D. 1995. "What Is the System in Systemic Reform?" *Educational Researcher* 24 (9): 11–17, 31.

Doyle, W. 1990. "Case Methods in Teacher Education." *Teacher Education Quarterly* 17 (1): 7–15.

EDC/EES (Education Development Center and Educational Extension Service of The Michigan Partnership for New Education). 1995. *Faces of Equity*. East Lansing, MI: Michigan State University Board of Trustees and The Michigan Partnership for New Education.

Elmore, R. 1995. "Structural Reform and Educational Practice." *Educational Researcher* 24 (9): 23–26.

———. 1996. "Getting to Scale with Good Educational Practice." *Harvard Educational Review* 66 (1): 1–26.

Fullan, M. 1993. *Change Forces: Probing the Depths of Educational Reform*. Bristol, PA: Falmer Press, Taylor-Francis.

Fullan, M., and M. Miles. 1992. "Getting Reform Right: What Works and What Doesn't." *Phi Delta Kappan* 73 (10): 744–752.

Fullan, M., and S. Steigelbauer. 1991. *The New Meaning of Educational Change*. New York: Teachers College Press.

Kagan, D. 1993. "Contexts for the Use of Classroom Cases." *American Educational Research Journal* 30 (4): 703–723.

Kleinfeld, J. 1992. "Learning to Think Like a Teacher." In *Case Methods in Teacher Education*, ed. J. Shulman, 33–49. New York: Teachers College Press.

Kleinfeld, J., and S. Yerian. 1995. Preface. In *Gender Tales: Tensions in the Schools*, ed. J. Kleinfeld and S. Yerian, v–x. New York: St. Martin's Press.

Merseth, K. 1992. "Cases for Decision Making in Teacher Education." In *Case Methods in Teacher Education*, ed. J. Shulman, 50–63. New York: Teachers College Press.

Miller, B., I. Kantrov, and J. Hunault. 1996. "Windows and Mirrors: Designing Video Cases to Promote Teacher Inquiry." Presented as part of a symposium, "Designing Innovative Video for Teachers' Professional Development." American Educational Research Association Annual Meeting, New York.

Shulman, J. 1992. Introduction. In *Case Methods in Teacher Education*, ed. J. Shulman, xiii–xvii. New York: Teachers College Press.

Shulman, J., and A. Mesa-Bains. 1993. Preface. In *Diversity in the Classroom: A Casebook for Teachers and Teacher Educators*, ed. J. Shulman and A. Mesa-Bains, v. Hillsdale, NJ: Research for Better Schools and Lawrence Erlbaum Associates.

Shulman, L. 1986. "Those Who Understand: Knowledge Growth in Teaching." *Educational Researcher* 15 (2): 4–14.

———. 1992. "Toward a Pedagogy of Cases." In *Case Methods in Teacher Education*, ed. J. Shulman, 1–30. New York: Teachers College Press.

Silverman, R., W. Welty, and S. Lyon. 1992. *Case Studies for Teacher Problem Solving*. New York: McGraw-Hill.

Style, E. 1988. "Curriculum as Window and Mirror." In *Listening for All Voices: Gender Balancing the School Curriculum*. Summit, NJ: Oak Knoll School.

Sykes, G., and T. Bird. 1992. "Teacher Education and the Case Idea." *Review of Research in Education* 18: 457–521.

Tyack, D., and W. Tobin. 1994. "The 'Grammar' of Schooling: Why Has It Been So Hard to Change?" *American Educational Research Journal* 31 (3): 453–479.

Wassermann, S. 1993. *Getting Down to Cases: Learning to Teach with Case Studies*. New York: Teachers College Press.